Enterprise Marketing Management

Enterprise Marketing Management

The New Science of Marketing

Dave Sutton and Tom Klein

WILEY

John Wiley & Sons, Inc.

Published by John Wiley & Sons, Inc., Hoboken, New Jersey.
Published simultaneously in Canada.

For general information on our other products and services please contact our
Customer Care Department within the U.S. at (800) 762-2974, outside the
United States at (317) 572-3993, or fax (317) 572-4002.

Wiley also publishes its books in a variety of electronic formats. Some content
that appears in print may not be available in electronic books. For more
information about Wiley products, visit our web site at www.Wiley.com.

ISBN 0-471-26772-4

Printed in the United States of America
10 9 8 7 6 5 4 3 2 1

For Whitney, Wheeler, and Maggie—D.S.

*For my scientist grandfather, Admiral John T. Hayward,
and for my salesman father, George.*—T.K.

CONTENTS

ACKNOWLEDGMENTS

This book is the result of relentless hard work on the part of many talented people. While conducting research for the book and developing content, we had the pleasure of meeting and working with many marketers and hearing their stories—many of which became the foundations for case studies in this book: Lisa Gregg at American Express, Tim Riesterer at Ventaso, and David Perry at Aspen Skiing Company.

We would like to thank everyone at Zyman Marketing Group for their dedication to bringing *Enterprise Marketing Management* to life with our clients across the globe. We would like to especially thank those colleagues that dedicated their personal time, of which there's never enough, to the book. They've added content, been there to think through new ideas, advanced their own theories, and helped us to bring it all together. Thanks to Ric Alvarez, Art Ash, David Cross, Leanne Fesenmeyer, Linda Michaels, Michael Sinclair, Dave Singleton, and Jon Stewart for their energy, ideas, and general passion for great marketing. And, thanks to Denise Cowden and Veda Sammy for their creativity and patience in helping to develop and organize both the written and graphical content. Even though marketing is a science, they've helped us apply art where it's necessary to help us communicate more clearly. And finally, even books about marketing need to be marketed. A special thanks to Chris Baradel and Linda Rondinelli for their help in applying all of the principles held within in order to get this book into your hands.

Thanks to our agent, Jim Levine, for getting the project moving and helping along the way with his insights. Also, thanks to our editor at Wiley, Airié Stuart, for working with us to refine the manuscript and for keeping the project on track.

A special thanks to Jay Busbee for both his creativity and his patience in learning our business, and Marie Pechet and Jonathan Baskin for working closely with us to refine our ideas and content.

We owe both an apology and a debt of gratitude to numerous friends and family members who read our work, gave us honest feedback and, most important, put up with us during the long nights and weekends we committed to getting this book completed amid our already hectic work schedules.

And, of course, a very special thanks to Sergio Zyman for giving us the inspiration to put our perspective into print. His spirited guidance and infectious passion for marketing have been and continue to be invaluable.

FOREWORD

Sergio Zyman

Since I wrote *The End of Marketing as We Know It* a few years ago, I have grown more convinced than ever that all of the principles it contains are true and continue to be true. Companies and organizations alike are adopting a scientific, disciplined approach to marketing. It's either because they realize that they need to in order to grow their business or because they are forced to do so by their customers or consumers who are not buying as much of their products as they used to. One of the most powerful distinctions that I revealed in that book was the fact that marketing is not an art—it is a science. Of course, there are artistic elements in some of the things that marketers do, but marketing itself is not an art, and it's not mysterious. It's about as mysterious as finance. You need to start with strategy and execute with discipline.

The first book was all about helping business leaders come to this realization and then develop strategies to help them get to where they want to go. Over the past few years we rapidly built our marketing strategy consulting business, Zyman Marketing Group, to help business leaders at some of the largest companies in the world understand my principles, develop a strategy, and get into action in the market. And, you know? It works.

We learn with every client, with every project, and we pass on our knowledge to our new clients.

Enterprise Marketing Management: The New Science of Marketing, which has been written by two of the senior members of Zyman Marketing Group, Dave Sutton and Tom Klein, demystifies marketing into a scientific discipline at the next level of detail. The book builds on the principles and practices that I outlined in *The End of Marketing as We Know It,* but it goes on to answer the difficult questions associated with implementing these principles and scientific practices within a business—revealing the implications for your business processes, information technologies, performance measures, jobs, skills, organization, and even culture. This book answers the questions that many people asked after they read *The End of Marketing as We Know It.* Yeah, that makes a lot of sense, but how do I get it done?

This is truly the ideal companion book to *The End of Marketing as We Know It.* It is the playbook that allows business leaders to begin transforming their marketing function and accelerating to realize business results by applying my principles in a systematic and logical way. This systematic and logical way has a new name: *enterprise marketing management.*

INTRODUCTION:
ENTERPRISE
MARKETING MANAGEMENT

Thousands of books have been written to try to explain how to go about the business of marketing. Most of them describe in a very basic way how to use tools like advertising or promotions or trade shows to drive your business.

This isn't one of those books.

What has been left out of the dialogue is that most marketers have been off on their own island for years, while the rest of the company (and the economy) has been transformed by the information revolution.

We have been active participants in the creative destruction this information revolution has wrought through our client work over the past decade. It has transformed nearly every business discipline.

We worked with the originators of reengineering, Michael Hammer and Jim Champy, to "fundamentally rethink and radically redesign business processes to achieve dramatic improvement" (*Reengineering the Corporation,* Harper Business, 1993). These efforts were a precursor to the implementation of enterprise resource planning (ERP) systems that completely changed the traditional functions of finance, operations, logistics, and human resources (HR).

Next we worked with one of the earliest implementers of Siebel's customer relationship management (CRM) software, which radically redefined and brought a high level of discipline to sales and customer service.

Now we have the opportunity to work with one of the world's top marketers, Sergio Zyman, to create and implement brand strategies for the biggest, most famous brands on the planet.

Given our experience across all business disciplines, we've noticed that marketing has, to date, avoided the sea change brought about by the information revolution. Indeed, over and over again, we see that it's this gap between marketing and the rest of the enterprise that is at fault for stagnating sales, high customer attrition, poor return on CRM and marketing investments, and overall poor financial results. While marketing is supposed to be charting the strategic course of the company, it's become the Luddite laggard when it comes to putting information to work to sell more.

The way to address this gap is *enterprise marketing management* (EMM).

Enterprise because this approach to marketing is simply too important to be left only to marketing. What could be more important to your company's success than understanding how to use every resource, not just the traditional levers of the marketing mix, to drive your company's sales and profits higher?

Marketing because, after all, this approach is still focused on understanding and developing a *market* and applying those traditional big levers of marketing, segmentation, and differentiation.

Management because this pragmatic, data-driven approach requires marketing to take more responsibility and interact much more extensively with the rest of the company. The notion of what makes up the brand simply *can't* be locked up between the ears of a few people in a little department called marketing. It has to be unleashed and managed across every person who interacts on the brand's behalf with any customer.

From the smallest local business to sprawling global enterprises, it's the end of the *art of marketing* and the beginning of the *new science of marketing*. Gone are the esoteric theories of marketing as a creatively driven endeavor. Now is the time for an analytical method that focuses on selling, plain and simple. Marketing isn't about awards; it's about results—and this book will help you get them.

A constant flow of relevant information is more important than any campaign. It's the only thing a marketer has to guarantee that every marketing asset and employee communicates the optimal messages and delivers the optimal benefits to drive sales and profits higher. You can't simply hand off this role to your ad agency.

If you're ready to step up to the plate to integrate real marketing discipline across your enterprise, you've got the right book in your hands. Ready to admit that your company needs to go to marketing boot camp to learn how to develop a disciplined, scientific approach to driving your sales and profits higher with every resource—your brands, your people, your stores, your trucks, your *anything?* Keep reading.

From a financial perspective, this enterprise marketing management isn't another method of spending more money than you're bringing in. Marketing's longstanding tradition of freewheeling, feel-good spending comes to an end with enterprise marketing management. From here on out, marketing will make investments, not gambles, and will make every effort to determine the return on those investments.

By pulling marketing out of its dark ages and committing to a more scientific approach, you will have the opportunity to put your company ahead of the pack, not just by spending your money wisely, but also by embracing all of the elements of an information-driven company. You can be at the vanguard of nothing short of a business revolution. And without a doubt, you'll be selling more—because at the end of the day, that's exactly what every marketer wants.

This book is organized in such a way that you can start at the beginning and read it straight through, or you can focus on the individual chapters appropriate to your situation. You may notice that we had to make up a few hypothetical cases along the way to demonstrate the marketer's scientific method. If you think about it, this should come as no surprise. Not many enterprises think about their marketing in this way, so there aren't a lot of great examples out there. The good news: You've still got time to change, embrace the new science of marketing, and assume a leadership position in the markets where you compete. (You may become a case for the next edition!)

The www.MarketingScientists.com web site can serve as a resource for you to continue your journey toward putting enterprise marketing management in place once you've finished this book. On the site you will find the following:

~ Contact information (access to marketing scientists)
~ New presentations/speeches (the science is always evolving)
~ Marketers' scientific methods
~ Newsletter sign-up

Each chapter includes at least one case study of the theories introduced. The companies outlined herein represent all sorts of industries, large and small, new and old. And they're not all positive case examples—sometimes it can be just as helpful to see what you're *not* supposed to do. Finally, at the end of each chapter are key approaches to try in your own company.

Enterprise marketing management is empowered by your desire to do whatever is necessary to drive profits higher. The desire alone won't suffice, though. You have to rethink how marketing should work in the information age. So, let's get going.

PART I

Run Brands as Businesses, Not as Campaigns

1

MARKETING IS NOT AN ART— IT IS A SCIENCE

Marketing is all about creativity, right? Mining idea space for inspiration that will connect with customers? Seeking that perfect message that will resonate so deeply with customers that they'll rush right out and buy your product?

Guess again. As Sergio Zyman pointed out in his first book, *The End of Marketing As We Know It?* (Harper Business, 1999) marketing is a science, not an art. And if you spend your time thinking of marketing as nothing but a creatively based endeavor, you're going to have a lot of ideas—but not a lot of customers.

This isn't the science of your old chemistry lab in high school. Many marketers chose marketing precisely because it involves interaction with some of the most creative people in our society— copywriters, advertising creatives, graphic artists. Marketers do tend to have an eye for how things should look, an ear for language, a deep and penetrating understanding, and zest for their cultural metaphor. There's absolutely nothing wrong with that.

However, every yin deserves a yang. The marketer's role simply can't consist of fawning or mindless meddling in the creative enterprise du jour. First and foremost, a marketer is a businessperson. It's indeed the responsibility of the marketer to bring a healthy portion of intellectual and process discipline to these investments in what are often creative exercises. It's this discipline that is at the heart of enterprise marketing management (EMM) and the new science of marketing.

To begin, a quick review of some of the terminology of science, starting with the dictionary definition:

sci·ence *n.*
1. The observation, identification, description, experimental investigation, and theoretical explanation of phenomena.
   a. Such activities restricted to a class of natural phenomena.
   b. Such activities applied to an object of inquiry or study.
2. Methodological activity, discipline, or study: He's got mowing the lawn down to a science.
3. An activity that appears to require study and method: the science of purchasing.
4. Knowledge, especially that gained through experience.

Now, the real-world definition: *science* refers to the way we explain the world around us, whether it's what's happening right now, what's happened up to this point, or what will happen if we take (or fail to take) certain actions. Centuries ago, science explained that the earth revolves around the sun, and not vice versa—correctly, accurately, and in the face of prevailing belief.

It's this facet of science—the ability to peer beyond the everyday, to ask questions and keep asking—that applies to marketing. What theories do you use to explain why things are the way they are? Why isn't your company selling more, more profitably, and more rapidly turning out new products? Why can't you get your stock price any higher? The theories—or, perhaps, rationalizations—that answer these questions constitute your understanding of your market and the actions of your business within that market.

Chances are, you already possess a significant degree of scientific knowledge about your current business, and you may even have a few theories of your own. The trouble is, too many theories are like old wives' tales—stories repeated so often, and with such conviction, that they take on the aura (and influence) of fact. Your company might have numerous theories about why things are the way they are, but few companies have taken the steps necessary to validate these theories. The need for validation will come into play later in this book, focusing on the use of your own customers (or target customers) to develop the value proposition for your brand. The question you need to answer is: How do you determine what benefits actually drive your customers to buy?

Start with a hypothesis about what you hope and expect to achieve with your marketing. For marketers, the usual hypothesis runs along these lines: Will this campaign/activity/initiative help us sell more? Within that overall framework are dozens of smaller, more focused questions, including these:

~ How do I increase share without cutting prices?
~ How do I get products to market faster?
~ How do I beat a competitor that's 10 times my size?
~ How do I close deals faster?
~ How do I reposition my brands against my competition?
~ How do I develop new products that win?
~ How do I segment my markets to sell more?
~ How do I differentiate what I sell when I'm in a commodity market?

Each one of these questions leads up to the big one: Does this action actually help me sell more of what I have to more customers at higher margins? Before you get to that point, however, you have to prove a number of hypotheses along the way, which will help you gain a greater understanding of your market. In other words, the better your overall understanding of your market, the more likely you are to sell more with your marketing programs.

Think back to your elementary school science classes, and you'll remember a technique called the scientific method, a means to prove or disprove hypotheses by following these steps:

1. Observe some aspect of the universe.
2. Invent a theory that is consistent with what you have observed.
3. Use the theory to make predictions.
4. Test those predictions by experiments or further observations.
5. Modify the theory in the light of your results.
6. Return to step 3, and continue as needed.

Easy enough . . . if you're testing, say, the boiling point of water. But how does this relate to marketing? Consider the opportunities that open up when applying the scientific method to a tangible marketing possibility:

1. **Observe some aspect of the universe—that is, your market.**   For example: The average age of the population is increasing.
2. **Invent a theory that is consistent with what you have observed.**   The average age of my buyer is increasing.
3. **Use the theory to make predictions.**   Older buyers are more health oriented and would respond to marketing programs and products that address health concerns.
4. **Test those predictions by experiments—in this case, marketing programs—or further observations.**   Launch health-oriented products and marketing programs.
5. **Modify the theory in the light of your results.**   Get results and learn!
6. **Go to step 3, and repeat until you've mastered this ability to repeat successful experiments to achieve your desired results.**

Are you addressing issues this way? Are you applying the scientific method to your marketing?

Everyone applies this method at a certain level, even if it's as simple as determining another way to get to work when the traffic's heavy. But marketers traditionally must figure out how the scientific method applies to their work while suffering with one hand tied behind their back. And sometimes they've done poorly with the hand they have left to them.

Marketing tends to function in an information vacuum—or an information disconnect. Think of it like gambling. When the dot-coms spent millions on Super Bowl advertising—the corporate equivalent of living in a trailer and gambling one's life savings—is that really a better investment than placing all that money on red and spinning the roulette wheel?

Gambling away dollars like this means your marketing isn't based on any particular aspect of the market. Gambling away dollars doesn't proceed logically from a measured observation of the universe around you. And reverse-engineering science to fit the results doesn't excuse the haphazard strategy of shotgun-style marketing.

If you're not applying the scientific method, what you're really doing is just gambling, nothing more. This isn't to say you won't hit a few winners along the way—chances are that you'll come up aces once in a while. But the odds are always against you: Play long enough, and you'll be flat out of chips.

PUTTING SCIENCE IN PLAY

So science explains what's happening (in your markets, with your customers), and the scientific method provides an approach to help you understand how to expand your knowledge and increase your control of what's happening. You're a marketer with products and services to sell. Your market represents your specific field of expertise, your historical business results, and information represents the science of your company—that is, everything you've learned to date—and your day-to-day efforts involve constant experimentation to learn more. With all this in your corner, you've got the opportunity to use this collective knowledge to develop and implement winning strategies.

Marketers have had decades of opportunity to do business this way, but a few speed bumps have cropped up along the way:

~ A lack of timely, relevant customer insights to define a brand's value proposition and drive brand decision making and investments
~ An inability to translate this value proposition into specific actions, both in traditional media and company-wide, to build an end-to-end brand experience with targeted customers
~ A lack of integration and accountability in action on relevant customer insights across key enterprise constituencies such as marketing, sales, service, manufacturing, finance, human resources (HR), information technology (IT), and so forth, to increase the profitability of the business

This kind of fancy marketing-speak tends to make most people's eyes glaze over—even those of experts in the field—but it delineates a fairly logical process. Marketers don't need fancy degrees, milewide skill sets, or reams of experience to succeed. All that's required is a simple focus on the best way to get your goods in the hands of your customers—and their money in yours. Think of it this way. Marketers often fail in three key categories: those with (1) the inability to use their knowledge of their customers to position their brands; (2) the inability to put their brands to work beyond traditional media; and (3) the inability to build necessary customer-facing processes with supporting organization, culture, and information for brand management.

RUN BRANDS AS BUSINESSES, NOT AS CAMPAIGNS

Each one of these stumbling blocks requires further examination, and succeeding chapters will explain more about how to address them. First you must recognize that your brands aren't these things that sit over in a corner and get talked about only by your marketers. Your brands *are* your business. If your company is guilty of any of the following:

~ Thinking of a brand as a cute logo, a spiffy tag line, or maybe a whiz-bang package
~ Going overboard and creating a new brand name for everything, but not having anywhere near enough money to actually make the brand name meaningful in the minds of your customers
~ Continuing to organize and track the business (How much did we sell? How much did we invest?) only on basic product categories or, even worse, by person (Bill's P&L, Joan's P&L) instead of by brands (brand-specific P&Ls)

Then you have plenty of work to do.

The first step on the road to enterprise marketing management is to think of and *run your brands as businesses*. Brands are much more than marketing campaigns, advertisements and logos. Don't give them any less respect than you would reserve for your divisions or departments of today. If you don't bring a brand-centric approach to the way you think about and manage your business, you will never get beyond square one.

Once you've decided to run your brands as businesses, the most basic problem that you will face is that your company probably has not learned how to use knowledge of its customers to position its brands. Certainly, there are shelves full of books on the subject, but this idea of positioning brands for some reason remains elusive for many companies. If you need to know the specific nuts and bolts of how to position brands to drive sales and profits, keep reading. Companies seem almost defiant in their preference to stick with their current guesswork instead of developing a deep understanding of the benefits that will really drive their customers to buy. In other words, the communication of what specific benefits has a causal relationship with more sales? Can you answer this for your brands? These benefits should be organized into a *brand architecture* that clearly fleshes out the value the company creates and the key emotional and functional benefits it must communicate consistently to sell more products and services.

In many instances, through no fault of their own, companies just don't know what marketing is supposed to do or be. Because real marketers are rare ducks who flock together in companies that spend big bucks on advertising, most companies do not even have true marketers running the show. Scratch the surface of most marketers at nearly any large company, and you'll often find refitted salespeople, trained in a completely different discipline. There's absolutely nothing wrong with being a great salesperson or a great engineer or a great information technologist. There is something wrong with pretending that there's no real science to marketing. You wouldn't expect your top salesperson to instantly know how to manage the logistics for your warehouses. Nevertheless, companies continue to put untrained marketers in positions where they're supposed to know something about how to put brands to work to drive sales and profits higher. It's no wonder marketing is in such a fragmented state. Part of bringing a more scientific approach to marketing is making sure you have real scientists running the laboratory—but that's a topic for later.

This inability to leverage customer insights extends beyond using customer knowledge to create a compelling brand architecture. Enterprise marketing management has also been inhibited from taking hold by the fact that marketing in general has remained separate from the information flow of the rest of the company. The information revolution has absolutely transformed the way business is done around the world. However, in most cases, marketing has experienced this revolution from the sidelines. That's not exactly a revelation, but the fact that marketing still hasn't made use of all available technology means the revolution's not yet over.

Nearly every company has pulled together all its information into easily accessible, accurate, integrated databases, so that nearly any person in the company can view information about transactions, customers, and products, all in real time. It's this uniform view of information across a company that's new.

Like every new technology, these systems break down into some neat three-letter acronyms. Think of this as some just-in-time learning:

CRM—customer relationship management. A category of enterprise-wide software applications that allow companies to manage every aspect of their relationship with a customer. The aim of these systems is to assist in building lasting customer relationships—to turn customer satisfaction into customer loyalty. Customer information acquired from sales, marketing, customer service, and support is captured and stored in a centralized *database*. The system may provide *data-mining* facilities that support a sales *opportunity* (a.k.a. *pipeline*) *management system.*

These systems help answer questions like: Are we going to hit our sales target this quarter? Which deals have to close in order to do so? Who was the last person to visit customer X?

ERP—enterprise resource planning. A category of enterprise-wide software applications that are designed to support and automate the core business processes of medium and large businesses. This may include manufacturing, distribution, personnel, project management, payroll, and financials. ERP systems are generally accounting-oriented information systems for identifying and planning the *enterprise*-wide resources needed to take, make, distribute, and account for customer orders. ERP systems were originally extensions of material resource planning (MRP) systems, but have since widened their scope.

These systems help answer questions like: Where's my order? What are the financial results?

SCM—supply chain management. These software applications provide an enterprise with oversight of materials, information, and finances as they move in a process from supplier to manufacturer to wholesaler to retailer to consumer. SCM applications involve coordination and integration of these flows both within and among companies. It is said that the ultimate goal of any effective SCM system is to reduce inventory (with the assumption that products are available when needed). There are two main types of SCM software: planning applications and execution applications. *Planning applications* use advanced algorithms to determine the best way to fill an order. *Execution applications* track the physical status of goods, the management of materials, and financial information involving all parties.

These systems help answer questions like: What is available to promise to customers? Where are the products in the supply chain? What is the best way to expedite and deliver this order?

While the rest of the company has largely become integrated thanks to ERP, SCM, and CRM initiatives, marketing remains the island within the enterprise. This inability to leverage company and customer information—the second most valuable asset of the company (the most valuable being the brand, of course)—has made much of the new science of marketing almost impossible to realize. Once marketers get in step, true optimization will be possible.

Thus, the role of marketers should be to inform decision making across the enterprise as the owners of the *brand experience*. For example, marketing may suggest a reduction in a production forecast or a change in the promotion calendar, which in turn will impact the focus of the sales force—all in support of the needs and wants of the target customers.

The good news is that knowing what these systems can do for you will help you adapt to the new science of marketing. The bad news is that you can't afford to stand still any longer because these technologies are creating great opportunities for you.

MANAGE YOUR BRAND, NOT YOUR CUSTOMER

Leveraging customer data to build a brand architecture and plugging marketing in to the rest of the enterprise represent the right first steps. The next piece missing from the puzzle is to take the value proposition spelled out in the brand architecture and translate it into a productive and profitable brand experience for your customers.

Creating this brand experience means that marketing must develop the specific content, functionality, and messages that are delivered at each customer touch point. These touch points can be anything from a meeting with a salesperson to clicks on a web site.

The brand experience addresses all aspects of the way your company interacts with your customer, including downstream, postpurchase interactions concerning how to use or service what you sell.

REINVENT YOUR BUSINESS, NOT JUST COMMUNICATIONS

The final reason that EMM has failed to take hold is that companies simply haven't constructed the processes or organization required to build and manage a brand experience across every customer touch point.

From a process perspective, marketing still functions as if it existed in a vacuum, separate from nearly every other financial decision made in the company. Enterprises that agonize over whether to build a factory to fill additional capacity, whether to make that next technology upgrade, or even whether to buy a company to fill out its product line routinely make marketing decisions that make it appear as if they'd left their spreadsheets at home. As Sergio Zyman rightly notes, marketing is an investment, pure and simple, not an optional expense or a luxury. The processes that surround executing and tracking a marketing program should mirror the processes that are put in place to ensure that every investment earns the required return.

This level of discipline just doesn't exist in most marketing departments today. Many marketers characterize hard-facts duties such as the size of the marketing budget or the determination of return on investment (ROI) as too difficult or not worth the effort. This sort of behavior only contributes to the reputation of marketers as profligate spenders without any notion of financial responsibility.

Customer insights drive brand decision making and marketing investments. The term *investment* (rather than *expense*) connotes the way that marketing should function. Just as you should think twice before you pour your 401(k) funds into high-risk tech stocks or your neighbor's latest start-up idea, so should you think carefully before you spend your marketing budget on a long-shot gamble when you likely can find more solid marketing investments out there.

It's worth noting at this point that the customer insights that drive decision making must be both relevant and timely. Compiling such information is an enormous challenge for nearly every company on the planet, but it's a necessary burden. It's critical that you understand the amount of marketing investment required to generate business with your target customers, as well as the amount of the return from doing business with those customers over time.

Consider a marketing investment profile, as noted in Figure 1.1. This profile indicates the timing of the investment and the timing of the return, which in turn lets you monitor both the incremental and the cumulative ROI for a specific marketing initiative. It offers an immediate snapshot of the validity of the marketing investment.

Creatively minded marketers shouldn't let all this science and investment talk scare them. The art of marketing is also more important than ever. The creative genius that drives brilliant marketing remains a critical part of everything that a marketer does. But the left-brain aspects of marketing—investment management

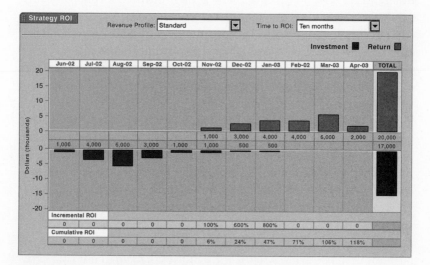

FIGURE 1.1   Marketing Investment Profile

and other hard-numbers processes—can be enabled and strengthened by information technology. Furthermore, new marketing technology applications can give marketers the freedom to focus on brilliant creative ideas to deliver on strategy. The marketing investment approach, combined with creative drive, gives marketers an even greater ability to build brand and drive value for their company.

As Sergio Zyman indicates in *The End of Advertising As We Know It*, brands stand at the center of everything that marketing does. The EMM approach to marketing indicates that the way to evaluate a brand is based on how much it sells, not on the kind of finger-to-the-wind approach that might show up on the front page of *USA Today*. Brands are only valuable as long as they sell. (Ask department store Montgomery Ward about the value of branding in and of itself these days.) Microsoft is a great brand not because of some intrinsic value, but because Microsoft sells an awful lot of software.

Brands are powerful and valuable only when they deliver sales. Brands that don't sell are just taking up shelf space. Thus, EMM describes how to build a brand experience that results in sales. A brand experience encompasses everything customers think about when they think about your brand, no matter how they're interacting with it.

Traditionally, marketing has focused on only the front end of the relationship. It's almost like a commitment problem—most marketers today are so focused on "dating" that they don't know what to do after they've closed the deal. And marketers who aren't able to craft a compelling enough brand experience will see their "dates" jumping ship as soon as something new and interesting—or maybe just a tad cheaper—comes along.

It's also worth noting that having a brand experience that just feels good isn't worth anything. If your campaign's not generating money for your company, you won't last very long in the spotlight. This is the dangerous side of the current CRM trend—focusing on the fun side of branding at the expense of hard science is a recipe for disaster.

For too long, marketing has suffered behind the unseen walls that exist between marketing and all the other departments of the company. How can a company develop a brand experience for its customers that encompasses traditional selling and marketing activities, as well as operations and service, when it's almost impossible to get marketing and sales departments to speak with one another—much less marketing and operations?

You've got a lot to tackle if you're going to put EMM into place in your company. You have to develop a deep understanding—a scientific understanding—of your market and your customers. Only then can you adequately develop your brand's value proposition, as well as the right way to communicate it to your customers to make them buy your product and not just "feel good" about it.

> *Next, you have to translate that value proposition framework—the brand architecture—into specific actions across the entirety of the brand experience cycle: need-evaluate-buy-use-support.*

In other words, marketing has to move beyond its traditional reliance on third-party media, such as TV or print ads, and put all of its customer touch points to work as sales drivers. Not only is this cheaper, but it's the only way to learn over time while building your own franchise that can't be duplicated by your competitors.

Finally, marketing processes, and everything that makes them run, must be rethought from the inside out. Implementing a scientific approach to marketing cannot be accomplished with just a sheaf of studies or brainstorming. You have to put real changes in place, bringing together organization, culture, incentives, and information technology to make building and retaining a brand experience possible. Financial discipline and scientific rigor must take hold across every marketing decision. Otherwise, you'll stay stuck in the past, gambling away your marketing dollars.

The first step on the journey to EMM: Know your brand.

2

ARCHITECT YOUR BRAND

According to Sergio Zyman in *The End of Marketing As We Know It,* "Every brand has to have a positioning strategy and everything you do with regard to that brand must communicate it." He goes on to assert that brands are the most critical value-producing asset for the enterprise and that they are the only true source of preference and differentiation for your business from your competition. Therefore, it should come as no surprise that the starting point for enterprise marketing management is to develop a deep understanding of your target customers and architect your brands to secure strategic market positions that will drive sustained profitability for your business.

A simple example of a well-architected brand is M&M's candies. First are the brand attributes: milk chocolate with a candy crunch. Next is the primary functional benefit: "melts in your mouth—not in your hands." Finally you have the key emotional benefit: fun, family-enhancing experience. It's well architected because it works. In this chapter you will learn how to *dimensionalize* your brand, to configure the building blocks of brand adoption, to assess your brand equity against that of your competition, and to bring it all together in a brand architecture that can be used to position your business to achieve sustained profitability.

A short refresher in building a brand architecture is called for. However, as you're developing your brand architecture, don't be constrained to thinking about benefits that can be delivered only by traditional communication vehicles. Expand your benefit exploration to include benefits that could be delivered on or communicated by everyone from your company's truck drivers to your customer service reps. At every step and at every interaction, your customer forms an opinion of your brand and builds a rationale for whether to buy or not buy. Why leave that up to chance?

What Does Your Brand Say about You?

Every brand that's ever had the slightest measure of success has managed to communicate its company's core beliefs and attitudes— what the company stands for—to its target customers. Brands allow you to clearly define and communicate what you stand for, whether you're the lowest-cost provider, the most innovative, the best total solution, the preferred choice, or whatever. But you've got to decide what your brand stands for and communicate that value proposition (e.g., Wal-Mart's "Always Low Prices" or FedEx's "Absolutely, positively overnight") effectively and repeatedly. It's not good enough simply to run a quality business—you've got to let everyone know what sets you apart from the pack.

Furthermore, you need to maintain constant control over the perception of your brand, because if you don't, it's a sure bet that the competition will. The brand should help customers navigate their way to your business even in the face of competing enticements. Under ideal circumstances, brands can even put customers on autopilot, bringing them back again and again to your door without them even considering your competitors. Keeping a tight rein on your message ensures that your competition doesn't siphon off your customers.

Consider the unfortunate case of Kmart, an extremely well-known brand with diffused brand messages—low prices in the form of blue-light specials, a high/low pricing strategy driven by advertising circulars, some desirable brands like Sesame Street and Martha Stewart, all delivered in a mix of retail locations (older, more urban neighborhoods than Wal-Mart's locations). After nearly a decade of turnaround efforts, Kmart's sales have declined and its cost structure rose to the point of driving the company into bankruptcy. Why?

Because Kmart forgot or, even worse, lost the central message of its brand. It confused its target customers, and its competitors (Wal-Mart and Target) took control of its message. The competition changed the rules of the low-price game, changing it from a promotion based strategy (using periodic specials) to an everyday framework. Wal-Mart carved out this everyday low-price positioning, invested heavily in the infrastructure to establish a superior cost position (even when it was at the same sales levels, Wal-Mart was overwhelmingly more efficient than Kmart), and then executed flawlessly, over and over again.

Target, wishing to stay out of Wal-Mart's way, has aimed higher, delivering to more upscale buyers who still want great prices but don't want to make the perceived sacrifice in quality and selection that Wal-Mart can sometimes imply. Target (said with a French accent, accompanied by a sassy and hip attitude) can deliver what has been termed the "affordable luxury."

Kmart got caught in the squeeze play. It was too far behind in infrastructure investment to catch up to Wal-Mart once it was eclipsed in sales, and it didn't have the goods to deliver to Target's customers, either. Sure, Wal-Mart was more efficient—even in the mid-1990s when the stores had roughly equivalent sales. But Wal-Mart rapidly doubled and then tripled the sales of Kmart. Soon it occupied the most powerful position with vendors and not only could it execute more efficiently, it could purchase merchandise at lower prices than could Kmart.

Kmart lurched in the other direction, likely thanks to hiring new management from Target in the mid-1990s, by attempting to move into specialty retailing, such as Martha Stewart's Everyday line, at a time when it should have been vigorously repositioning its core brand. What chance do upscale brands like Martha Stewart Everyday stand in dirty, run-down, poorly merchandised stores in what Kmart's own management deemed as some of the least desirable shopping centers around the country? (See the Kmart case study later in this chapter.)

And just as you can't stand pat and let the competition overwhelm you, you also can't spread yourself too thin and be all things to all consumers. Kmart's more recent moves suggest that the brand had lost its way completely. The company attempted to emulate the everyday-low-price model with a "Blue Light Always" initiative, seeking the same target audience that Wal-Mart pursues.

But a family of four with an annual income of $50,000 has little interest in specialty products from Martha Stewart. The net result, from a consumer perspective, is confusion: Just what exactly does this company stand for? Nowadays baby boomers use Kmart as a cultural reference point demarcating the middle and lower classes. In other words, they wouldn't be caught dead shopping there.

The lesson has been brutal for Kmart, but instructive: You can't have a productive, profitable relationship with your customers unless you bring clarity to what you stand for. This applies to both your target customers and every other player in your competitive set. Your brand is the focal point, the repository for both the intrinsic and the extrinsic benefits associated with your offerings. If it's not clear in the minds of your customers, you're going to start taking on water quickly and may never recover.

> ***Do your customers know what your brand means?***

THE ARCHITECTURE OF A BRAND

Like a person, a brand has individual values, physical features, personality, and character. Like a story, a brand has characters, setting, and a plot. Like a friend, a brand offers a personal relationship, one that—in the best-case scenario—evolves as you do.

Given the great interest and potential reward in building a powerful, premium-earning brand, it is not surprising that there exists an array of theories, models, and techniques put forth by consultants, authors, and academicians, each purporting to be the final word on building and managing brands. The more complicated the theory is, the less likely it's any good. Building brands, like marketing itself, is a science, not an art. You don't need to contemplate the black arts or have to give your firstborn to Rumpelstiltskin. You can build a powerful brand by simply following the instructions described in this chapter.

The term *brand architecture* is actually the output of the brand-building exercise. It's a critical step in building a brand that provides you with everything you need to know to get your customers to buy more. From there, subsequent chapters will explain how you can use enterprise marketing management and its scientific approach to put the brand architecture to work across your enterprise.

A brand architecture, analogous to the architecture for a building, lays out the key elements of the brand in detail and reveals specific messages and important take-aways for the target audience.

> *A brand architecture can include emotional benefits, functional benefits, physical benefits, product attributes, occasion appropriateness, user imagery, and a variety of other intangibles.*

The brand architecture represents the structural integrity of the brand, delineating how it is built, how it works, and how the components fit together to deliver meaningful benefits to the consumer—just as a skyscraper's architecture does for the building (see Figure 2.1).

A brand architecture, grounded in the science of understanding why customers purchase and use products, provides direction about which combination of specific emotional and functional benefits can generate the greatest amount of customer purchase intent. Once

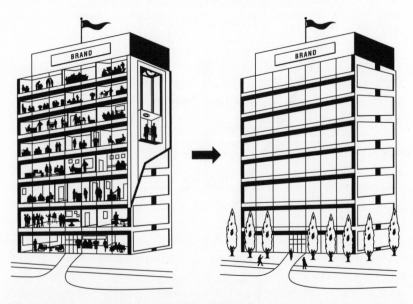

FIGURE 2.1   From Structural Integrity to External Façade of a Brand

completed, a brand architecture produces a strategic marketing framework visible to the entire organization. You can then use this framework to begin communicating and delivering these benefits to your customers.

KEY DIMENSIONS OF A BRAND ARCHITECTURE

So what makes a brand architecture tick? The key dimensions of a brand architecture are its foundational attributes (or product features), functional benefits, and emotional benefits (Figure 2.2). You can determine the structure of a brand architecture by focusing on the key purchase intent drivers—*the attributes or benefits that influence customers' overall decisions to purchase or use a product.*

Despite the concrete-sounding name, purchase intent drivers are often intangible qualities. Marketers can measure these drivers by

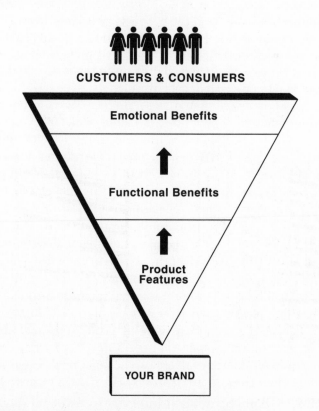

FIGURE 2.2   Dimensions of Brand Architecture

determining how much a given emotional benefit, functional benefit, or brand attribute *drives* a customer's desire to purchase a brand in a certain competitive frame. For instance, some soft drink consumers may prefer a clear drink over a caramel-colored cola; in that case, the "clear" attribute will be deemed a driver of purchase intent. Other consumers might care more for drivers such as taste, cost, or convenience, leaving the clear/caramel-color distinction aside.

It's important to note that drivers of customer purchase intent (the specific benefits that get customers to buy) are not always intrinsic to individual brands, but can be relevant to categories of competitors as a whole, providing opportunities to siphon volume from competitors. It's the reason that knockoffs or me-too versions of popular new products spring up almost immediately—the theory is, "It's worked for them, why not for us?" In a brand-savvy environment, once one brand sees that another has uncovered a driver of purchase intent, then it's only a short time until a copy appears.

So why bother with branding if it's just going to be copied in short order? The secret here is to, of course, keep up with the Joneses but also to put most of your effort in defining and *owning* that mix of benefits and attributes that is indeed difficult to replicate and that your company is uniquely capable of delivering.

The most compelling purchase intent drivers often reflect underlying emotional benefits associated with the competitive frame and the brand—which is why you so rarely see well-known products being described with basic product attributes or simplistic functional benefits. How often are Oreo cookies lauded for their chocolate flavor? What you often see are emotion-charged advertisements aimed at mothers, which focus on teaching your young child how to eat an Oreo (the dunk, the twist) as part of being a good mom (emotional benefit) and something of a rite of passage. These ads don't address the fact that Oreos are a better deal, pound for pound, than Pepperidge Farm cookies (a functional benefit). This emotional benefit is something that, according to many people, only a few snacks could offer. If a competitor launched a new product, how might it compete with Oreo's heritage and ability to deliver on specific emotional benefits?

While purchase intent drivers can be emotional benefits, functional benefits, or brand attributes, they're not all created equal (see Figure 2.3).

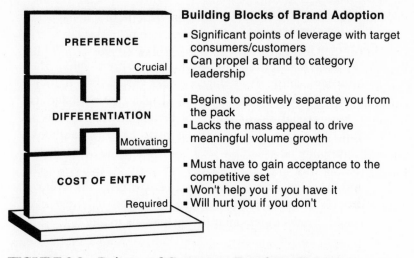

FIGURE 2.3   Drivers of Customer Purchase Intent

Cost-of-entry purchase intent drivers encompass the benefits that *any* brand must deliver to be considered a viable option. If you're a fast-food provider, you'd better be able to serve your customers their burgers and fries in a hurry. Everyone in the competitive frame can deliver these benefits; they're the minimum ante necessary to play the game. To determine the cost-of-entry benefits, you need to understand why consumers purchase *any* brand in the competitive frame and determine how your brand stacks up on these benefits.

Differentiation purchase intent drivers are the benefits that begin to positively separate you from the rest of the competition. These are capabilities or equities that you possess that others in the competitive set may not. Of course, these benefits may not appeal or be motivating to all customers in the target audience. Indeed, if these benefits are not of significant importance, they may remove you from customers' consideration—it doesn't matter how comfortable your minivan is, for instance, if someone's determined not to buy a minivan. More important, your distinct benefits may not be in the top of your consumers' minds and will require a certain amount of communication and education in order to induce purchase.

Preference drivers are benefits that can propel a brand to category leadership. These benefits are crucial in the minds of customers as they consider various brand alternatives in your competitive set. These types of benefits represent significant points of leverage with customers and can become the source of sustainable advantages. These may be as simple as a "buy American" consideration, or they may come about through extensive research and experience with a variety of competitors. Preference drivers are the trump card, the brand attributes that keep your customers coming back again and again.

BRINGING IT ALL TOGETHER IN A BRAND ARCHITECTURE

A brand architecture provides a strategic hierarchy of the brand's key dimensions and outlines the way in which each of the aforementioned drivers fits into the overall matrix. As a result, the brand architecture is the most crucial document in your entire marketing plan. In the simplest form, the brand architecture informs you which benefits will be most effective, which will be the least effective, and which will be ineffective at driving the purchase intent of your target consumers as portrayed in Figure 2.4. Consequently, it must guide all company activity related to the brand.

To better communicate and help you understand the elements of building a brand architecture, we've conjured the hypothetical Refreshing BeerCo from thin air. The beer category provides a great example because just about everyone can relate to it and has been faced with that challenging question from the barkeep, "What'll ya have?"

Consider the hypothetical brand architecture for Refreshing BeerCo shown in Figure 2.5. The Refreshing BeerCo brand is a repository for a set of product attributes, functional benefits, and emotional benefits, all of which combine to promote Refreshing BeerCo's image to its target customers. Some of these benefits and features are just the cost of entry for the beer category (e.g., great taste). Some of them are actually differentiators (e.g., "real beer-drinking experience"), and some have the potential to drive true

	FEATURES	FUNCTIONAL BENEFITS	EMOTIONAL BENEFITS
PREFERENCE			Most Effective
DIFFERENTIATION			
COST OF ENTRY	Least Effective		

FIGURE 2.4   Determining Effectiveness of Brand Positioning

preference for the Refreshing BeerCo brand (e.g., "turns any time into a special occasion"). This architecture can then be used to inform the content communications and investment decisions related to the entire marketing mix and every element of the brand experience. What are the key messages that we are sending? How

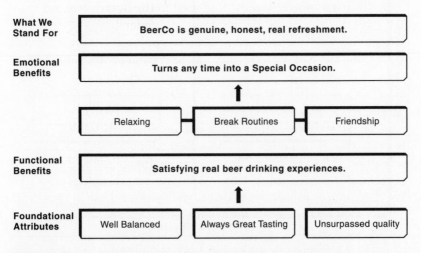

FIGURE 2.5   Refreshing BeerCo Brand Architecture

do these messages reinforce what Refreshing BeerCo stands for? Are we weighting messages appropriately or focusing too much attention on things that are just the cost of entry for the category? When properly used, the brand architecture becomes the ultimate tool for making sure that your tactics (e.g., marketing communications, promotions, pricing strategy) stay aligned.

BRAND EQUITY DRIVERS

Once you've got the basic framework of your brand architecture, it's time to figure out what you can do that no one else can, to establish the unique attributes that set you apart from your competitors. These brand equity drivers encompass the sets of benefits whereby your brand has an advantage over all others in your sphere. If no one brand holds a sustainable advantage, it's an open opportunity—nobody has enough sway to pull consumers one way or another. It's the high ground not yet taken—and the turf you should strive to conquer.

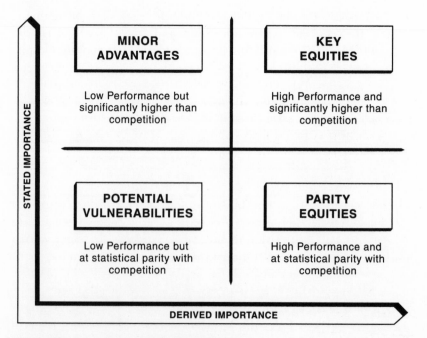

FIGURE 2.6   Brand Equity Drivers

Brand equity drivers include those shown in Figure 2.6 and are described as follows:

Key equity drivers are those that give you direct leverage against your competition. Quite simply, your business performance is higher than that of your competition, and you can use this strength to take new ground, building new equities in areas that were previously open opportunities.

Minor advantage drivers are those benefits whereby your brand rates are statistically stronger than the competition, but your business performance is actually lower than that of the competition. Your brand is intrinsically strong, even if your performance is weaker than that of your competition. And in this case perception is reality—if your target customers think you're a stronger company than your competition, in the long run, you will be.

Parity equity drivers come into play when your brand ratings are statistically equivalent to those of your competition, but you have a higher level of business performance. In this case, it's to your advantage to highlight your own strengths and your competitors' weaknesses.

Potential vulnerability drivers are those benefits whereby your brand rates at a statistical dead heat with the competition, but your performance is actually lower than that of your competitors. This is dangerous territory; it's only a matter of time before the competition seizes on this vulnerability—and reveals it to your target consumers.

A detailed analysis of Refreshing BeerCo's brand positioning found significant vulnerabilities in relation to the category's leader, Budweiser. However, Refreshing BeerCo possesses advantages over its competition in several key drivers. In other words, although there are parity equities with the category leader, there also exist open opportunities to take share from other competitors based on key drivers: brewed smooth, not watered down, never harsh or bitter, relaxing, refreshing (see Table 2.1). Accordingly, these drivers will form the backbone of the Refreshing BeerCo brand architecture.

Table 2.1   Refreshing BeerCo Competitive Equity Analysis

Relative "BeerCo" Ratings
Top Two Box Ratings by Brand Drinkers

Opportunistic Equities	Versus Budweiser	Versus Regional Competitor	Versus Mexican Import	Versus European Import
Brewed to be smooth	=	+	+	+
Genuine	=	+	+	+
Not watered down	=	+	+	=
Never harsh or bitter	=	=	=	+
Helps me relax	=	+	=	=
Maximum refreshment	=	+	=	—

(+) Key Equity (=) Parity Equity (–) Potential Vulnerability

HOW TO DEVELOP A BRAND ARCHITECTURE

Looking inward to help develop brand architecture is necessary, but it's only half the battle. Developing a brand architecture also requires a deep understanding of customer needs and wants. Such understandings must derive from quantitative data—that is, surveys of broad ranges of customers—rather than the qualitative data gained from focus groups. Analyzing the brand and its key competitors across a spectrum of potential consumers helps determine drivers, equities, and opportunities. Qualitative data is not typically sufficient to develop an appropriately thorough brand architecture.

However, as with so much in life, the devil is in the details. For your brand architecture to provide necessary insight, you've got to have specific information on the subtle but meaningful differences between brands. The amount of insight and ability to take action are directly proportional to the specificity of benefit statements and ratings of competitors.

Now, back to Refreshing BeerCo for more on how customer articulations reveal meaningful differences and provide direction. As Refreshing BeerCo developed its brand architecture, it uncovered literally thousands of different articulations of category- and brand-related attributes and benefits. In the area of taste alone, customers generated roughly 100 different expressions! With this level of detail, the analysis could distinguish among cost-of-entry taste attributes (great taste), equity taste dimensions (not watered down, genuine beer flavor), and open opportunity taste dimensions (energizing or invigorating taste). Refreshing BeerCo tested stated versus derived importance of various customer benefits, breaking down into the following six driver categories:

Credentials	Features of the beer and the history of the brewery
Individual	What drinking the product says about you and your personality
Transformation	How the product makes you feel while you're drinking
Social connections	The occasions and events associated with drinking beer
Responsibility	Addressing irresponsible consumption, drinking and driving, knowing your limits
Possibility	What is possible for you when consuming the product, positive outcomes

Based on the findings of this analysis, Refreshing BeerCo now had in hand a detailed understanding of which benefits were important to consumers (i.e., cost of entry), which ones were potentially motivating, and which were absolutely critical benefits that they had to headline (see Figure 2.7). In this way, specific strategic directions for consumer communication and creative promotion could be directly informed by consumer insights that correlated directly to consumer intent to purchase Refreshing BeerCo branded products—rather than gut intuition.

Analyses of Refreshing BeerCo's competitive frame also collected brand ratings across a wide variety of dimensions, including product attributes, functional benefits, emotional benefits, usage occasions, and user characteristics. Factor analysis summarized the different dimensions of the brand architecture—that is, the consumer's mental image of the brand. Regression analysis, using consumption frequency and brand preference measures as the dependent variables, identified the purchase intent drivers.

It's important to point out that this is a more complicated process than simply asking the people what they like. Direct questioning along stated importance or stated reason lines elicits purely

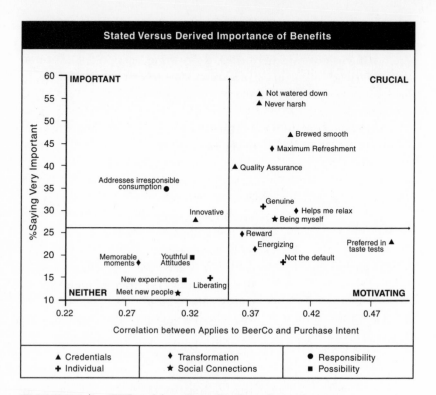

FIGURE 2.7   Refreshing BeerCo Purchase Intent Driver Analysis

rational—not emotional—responses and tends to favor existing, intrinsic product benefits. The correlation of behavior and attitudes will yield a far more comprehensive and valid insight into customers' behavior.

BRAND ARCHITECTURES DIFFER FROM BRAND TO BRAND

A brand architecture is a matrix of components unique to each brand within a competitive set—meaning that it's like a fingerprint, something that can't be copied and pasted from one brand onto another. Brands that are multidimensional (like, say, regular beer) have different architectures than brands that deliver more focused benefits, such as nonalcoholic beer. The architecture demonstrates how the various components come into play when different opportunities arise. The architecture must reveal appropriate purchase intent drivers, equity drivers, and opportunities across various markets, consumer segments, and usage occasions. Consider again the Refreshing BeerCo brand architecture for regular beer, shown in Figure 2.8.

Taste and authenticity hold the key equities for regular beer; consumers looking for "real beer taste" obviously gravitate to real beer. However, functional and emotional benefits are the key drivers of the category. Many consumers aren't just seeking beer for beer's sake; hence, they represent a higher level in the architecture. Most open opportunities reside in the arena of emotional refreshment. Thus, the architecture demonstrates how and why beer manufacturers can leverage the concepts of taste and authenticity to support and ultimately own emotional refreshment.

Naturally, the architecture for nonalcoholic beer brands is very different from the architecture for regular beer (see Figure 2.9). Nonalcoholic beer appeals to a much more homogeneous segment of consumers, and the reasons for drinking nonalcoholic beer are generally more similar across situations than is the case with regular beer.

Nonalcoholic beer's brand architecture depends on the linkage between the authentic taste of nonalcoholic beer and the self-respect component that arises from maintaining control over the drinking situation. This connection between intrinsics of taste and the extrin-

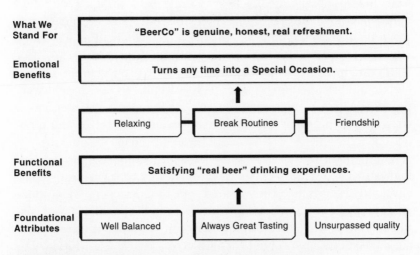

FIGURE 2.8   Regular Beer Brand Architecture

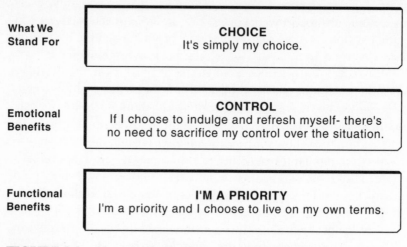

What We Stand For

CHOICE
It's simply my choice.

Emotional Benefits

CONTROL
If I choose to indulge and refresh myself- there's no need to sacrifice my control over the situation.

Functional Benefits

I'M A PRIORITY
I'm a priority and I choose to live on my own terms.

FIGURE 2.9   Nonalcoholic Beer Brand Architecture

sic equities is a unique aspect of brands in the nonalcoholic beer segment. Its extrinsic qualities don't even apply to regular beers; thus, nonalcoholic beer marketers must draw up their brand architecture from scratch or risk alienating potential core customers.

HOW BRAND ARCHITECTURE IS USED

Marketers use brand architecture as a means for bringing the brand to life via all elements of the marketing mix and across every customer touch point. It is the only way to guarantee a unity of appearances, appeals, and interactions. The key drivers focus energy on your strengths, open opportunities draw your notice to opportunities (obviously), and brand equities show you how to play to your best characteristics. With all of this scientific data in your corner, you now have a concrete starting point for defining and accentuating all of your product's benefits—however they might be presented to customers.

Remember that brand architecture forms the basis for developing operational strategies: How will you design your business so that absolutely everything orbits around your brand message? How does every element of your company contribute to the benefit of your customer? As you'll see in upcoming chapters, the brand architecture is a guidebook for operational changes across your enterprise: how to organize, train, and reward your personnel; how to design your selling and servicing processes; and how to implement various types of technology to support your customers throughout the process.

BRANDS AS BUSINESSES

Intuitively, we all know that successful businesses earn more than they spend. And the most successful businesses have built-up management processes and systems that help them continuously measure and monitor how much they earn and how much they spend. Today most companies structure themselves into business units (or product lines) or perhaps around the geographies where they sell their products. However, you should view your brands not as a part of the marketing department's budget but as discrete business units in and of themselves. Brands are your most valuable assets. In fact, brands are critical business assets (not unlike plant and equipment), each with its own characteristics, maintenance needs, profit and loss (P&L), and obligations for return on capital invested.

With this in mind, treating brands as businesses means applying the very basic elements of portfolio theory. Given the challenge of developing a brand architecture and then applying resources to bring it to life, are you suffocating under too many brands? Has your company proliferated brands, none with the adequate level of understanding or investment required to generate a return? The overwhelming majority of businesses suffer from one of these problems. Either they've not developed a firm enough understanding of their brand, the purchase intent drivers, the brand equity drivers, and the opportunities to be able to know *where* to invest marketing dollars, or, perhaps being lucky enough to have developed a sufficiently deep understanding of their customers to build a brand architecture, they may labor under the weight of too many brands without adequate investment.

It's very simple. Your investments determine which brand or brands live or die. Choose too many to support and none thrive. Make investments before building a brand architecture and you're doing little more than gambling.

A critical tenet of enterprise marketing management and its scientific approach is to let the facts speak for themselves. Don't let opinion or the status quo or your company's mythology dictate anything that you do. Stop and think: Why do we do it this way? What data actually support this decision?

Brands serve as a mental shorthand for customers looking to decide what to purchase. Marketing's primary purpose is to continuously optimize the levers of segmentation and differentiation for its brands because the target moves and—oh, by the way—so does the competition. Markets are inherently dynamic and changing. The right brand architecture one year may be the wrong one two years later.

Marketing must ensure that customers select your brand at every potential purchase occasion, through every desired channel. What does this mean for investments? How does it answer that age-old question of how much to spend on marketing? There's much more on these questions to come, but the short answer is to invest resources behind each and every brand to the point of diminishing returns. Again, this is where science comes into play in supporting your ability to run brands as businesses—if you can generate complete P&Ls for every brand and every activity, you can maximize your advertising and resource allocation efficiency, standing behind what works and effectively and efficiently getting rid of what doesn't.

The marketer's scientific method that comes at the end of each chapter will help you put management processes and systems in place to ensure that you are investing resources in marketing activities that generate a superior return on investment, while ensuring that your brands are being managed and run like the businesses they are.

Once you've architected your brand, you've taken the first and most critical step toward developing the deep understanding of the particular bundle of benefits that will drive your customers to buy and the equities that your brand owns and can leverage to drive sales and profits higher. So you've nailed down the "what." Read on for a much more detailed explanation of the "how."

CASE STUDY: Kmart

A BRAND THAT LOST ITS WAY—AND ITS CUSTOMERS

Background

Kmart's origins date back to 1897, when the S.S. Kresge Company launched a chain of five-and-dime stores. By the 1950s, Kresge was one of the largest general merchandise retailers in the United States. In 1962, Kresge gave birth to discount retailing in America when it opened its first Kmart store, and later it renamed the company after its leading retail brand.

During the 1970s, Kmart rode high, doubling its annual sales and stunning its competitors by opening as many as 250 stores a year. But the 1980s were not as kind, and Kmart began losing ground. While other retailers constantly upgraded their operations, Kmart did not make sufficient efforts to improve its merchandise or its accounting and inventory systems. Most visibly, Kmart did little to modernize the look of its stores.

Kmart established itself as the place to shop for discount merchandise—a branding that it accomplished a little too well, as it was unable to ever break from its cut-rate origins. Wal-Mart, also founded in 1962, experienced an initially slower growth curve but realized greater operational efficiencies along the way. In 1990, Wal-Mart surpassed Kmart as the largest discount retailer in the nation via a pervasive "We Sell for Less" slogan.

Ousted from its price leader position, Kmart plunged into an identity crisis from which it has yet to recover. The company had numerous other problems along the way, including location issues, inventory management problems, overreliance on promotions, management distractions, and heavy competition. But at the heart of it all, Kmart lost sight of its brand—and paid the price.

Strategic and Operational Blunders

Kmart used promotional tools such as the blue-light special and advertising circulars to pursue a classic high/low sales strategy. The company's objective was to lowball a few items in order to lure customers to the store, expecting they would fill the rest of their baskets with full-priced products. Naturally, those full-priced products needed to have as high a profit margin as possible. As far back as the early 1980s, Kmart had begun stocking designer labels with the dual purpose of squeezing more profits out of its high/low strategy and attracting a more affluent clientele.

But stocking designer labels at higher prices while touting low-priced promotions created a positioning dichotomy for Kmart. Analysts recently pointed out this disconnect in Kmart's simultaneous pursuit of a Martha Stewart partnership and a "Blue Light Always" initiative, but this kind of identity crisis has been pervasive for years. The question became: Is Kmart a destination for bargain hunters seeking a cheap can of beans or for upwardly mobile shoppers desiring measuring cups in Martha Stewart–approved colors?

Meanwhile, Wal-Mart steadfastly pursued a strategy of everyday low pricing in lieu of sales or promoting certain items. Experts predicted that the Wal-Mart strategy wouldn't work with coupon- and sales-addicted consumers—and the experts couldn't have been more wrong. Customers simply assumed that a cartful of items would cost less at Wal-Mart than anywhere else. The strategy enabled Wal-Mart to eliminate most newspaper advertising and simply to run image commercials boasting about low prices.

Kmart also failed to respond to its changing consumer base and heightened competition by literally repositioning itself. Having grown quickly in the 1970s, Kmart ended up with two-thirds of its store base in cities, while Wal-Mart and Target located in more suburban locations. Kmart did not respond adequately to the situation in the cities and to urban flight, leaving it with a low-growth customer base and little access to burgeoning numbers of suburban consumers. Attempts to rehabilitate the company's reputation for untidy, difficult-to-navigate stores proved fruitless.

Kmart's management also did a little too much shopping of its own. Between 1984 and 1991, Kmart aggressively dove into specialty retailing, adding several lines to its business, including Waldenbooks, Builders Square, Payless Drugstores Northwest, Pace Membership Warehouse, the Sports Authority, OfficeMax, and Borders bookstores.

Not surprisingly, a generalist like Kmart did a poor job of running these specialty retailers. By 1994–1995, Kmart flirted with bankruptcy, and it was forced to sell or spin off OfficeMax, the Sports Authority, Pace, and Borders. The company still pays $250 million a year in rent to guarantee 350 store leases for such spun-off chains as Builders Square, Borders, Sports Authority, and the defunct Pace Membership Warehouse Club.

The Pain of Heavy Competition

While Kmart's wounds are arguably self-inflicted, it's still worthwhile to take a closer look at its chief competitors, Wal-Mart and Target. Both did a far better job of preserving and enhancing their brands.

Between 1990 and 2000, Kmart saw its market share decline from 30 percent to 17 percent. Over the same period, Wal-Mart's market share increased from 30 percent to 55 percent, and Target's from 10 percent to 13 percent. According to analyst Kevin Murphy, of Gartner Inc., the Kmart stores that do well are in urban locations where there is no competition from a nearby Wal-Mart or Target. But in places where all three chains have stores, Kmart gets clobbered. Unfortunately for Kmart, there happens to be a Wal-Mart or a Target within seven minutes of 80 percent of Kmart stores. The profit picture is even more depressing for Kmart: In 14 years, Kmart has earned a total of $3.8 billion—a little more than Wal-Mart earns in six months.

Kmart's failure to definitively reposition itself after losing the price leadership battle left it squeezed out by these number one and number two retailers. Wal-Mart took the low ground on a national level in 1990 when it surpassed Kmart as the top discount retailer. Meanwhile, Target staked out a position just above Kmart, with chic merchandise at low prices.

Wal-Mart outsells Kmart by a margin of nearly two to one per square foot of store space. Wal-Mart also gained a huge efficiency advantage through automation and creative uses of information technology (IT). Target has found a niche selling to more upscale consumers than tend to frequent Wal-Mart, and it moves huge volumes of cheap chic clothes under its Mossimo brand and of housewares by the renowned Michael Graves.

Marketing Missteps

Most recently, Kmart experienced a series of marketing gaffes that accelerated its demise. The snowball began rolling when Kmart's marketing efforts failed to address its poor image with customers. Kurt Barnard, president of Barnard's Retail Consulting Group, said Kmart has made dramatic improvements in recent years but has failed to communicate those moves to customers.

One of the most confounding aspects of the Kmart situation is that the company already has the right tools to be competitive. Its product offerings include brands such as Martha Stewart, Disney, Sesame Street, and the Route 66 clothing line, but it has failed to play up these strengths with the public.

Kmart compounded its problems by choosing to go head to head with Wal-Mart, slashing prices under the "Blue Light Always" slogan and airing a "Dare to Compare" advertising campaign. But the strategy was an unmitigated failure—Wal-Mart promptly cut its prices, while Target sued for false advertising, forcing Kmart to take the ads off the air.

At the same time, the shift to the "Blue Light Always" promotion was too abrupt. Again, Kmart's branding had worked too well—its most loyal consumers were hooked on newspaper advertising circulars, thanks to years of training and reinforcement from Kmart marketers. Kmart vastly underestimated the degree to which these circulars drove traffic to its stores. Hoping to cut costs and shore up funds, Kmart simply sliced its circular advertising budget rather than weaning customers off the circulars.

The Latest Bold Move: Kmart Trades Red for Green!

Kmart is planning to change the color of its logo from red (which may be indicative of the state of its income statement) to green. The company has also been testing a new concept store in a few markets that features the new-color logo, wider aisles, better lighting, lower shelves, and directional icons to improve the shopping experience. The new store concept still features many of the same brand names, including Martha Stewart, Joe Boxer, Sesame Street, and Disney, but in the new format all of the high-end brands are positioned near the front of the store. The concept has been nicknamed the "Store of the Future"— perhaps as a promise to employees that there will be one. Despite desperate measures, Kmart's same-store sales continue to slide, finishing down nearly 12 percent in August 2002.

The final chapter of the Kmart story remains to be written. But because of the company's failure to preserve and enhance its brand, that chapter may not be long in coming.

MARKETER'S SCIENTIFIC METHOD: BUILDING A BRAND ARCHITECTURE

Following are the steps to take in order to build a brand architecture.

Step 1: Develop a Destination Statement

Before you charge ahead and start building your brand architecture, you've got to understand the destination you seek to reach with your brands and your portfolio of products in the long term as well as the short term. After all, if you don't know where you are headed, it's pretty difficult to get there. And the clearer the destination, the better you'll be able to develop a brand positioning and architecture that will get you where you want to go. First of all, you need to synthesize and articulate a *destination statement* for the brand to clearly answer the following:

~ What business do you seek to compete in for the long term?

~ Whom do you plan to sell to, now and in the future?

~ What will customers get from you that sets you apart from the alternatives?

~ How will customers benefit from your products and services?

~ How will customers think, feel, and act about your brands?

~ How will your business benefit as a result, in the long term?

The deliverable here must be a clear and concise destination statement for the brand that will provide focus for all the other activities required to develop the brand architecture.

Step 2: Conduct a Brand Assessment

Marketing does not consist of bells and whistles and cute ideas. What you do with your brands has to be born of your current reality, not plucked from the atmosphere because it sounds nice. In this step you must evaluate all the research, data, and insight you have to understand your brands, your customers, the competitive landscape, and the relevant developments that lie ahead. This step involves a thorough analysis and assessment of all your existing data and insight and should focus on the following:

~ Product characteristics, with key benefits and attributes

~ Business performance metrics

~ Category trends and insights

~ Competitive data and profiles

~ Customer/consumer research and insights

~ Pricing issues and analysis

In addition, you'll need to gather secondary research on the following:

~ Industry analysis and trends
~ Secondary research on customer usage and consumption habits
~ Expert interviews and surveys

The deliverable here will be a detailed *brand situation assessment* document that summarizes key findings in the following areas:

~ Market environment and opportunity
~ Customer/consumer targeting
~ Value proposition by target audience
~ Competitive analysis
~ Summary of data and insight gaps
~ Conclusions and indicated actions

Step 3: Develop Strategic Hypotheses

Everything that preceded this step prepares you to identify and flesh out the corridors that will ultimately lead to the optimal brand positioning and architecture for your product. An undisciplined process would start with this step—and would be akin to throwing mud against the wall and seeing what sticks. Instead, given the due diligence of the preceding steps, you will be operating in strategic areas that have a thoughtful basis for success.

Based on the conclusions and indicated actions from the brand situation assessment, you need to develop a comprehensive range of brand architecture hypotheses concerning the product attributes, functional benefits, and emotional benefits that may be most effective at motivating usage and consumption of your brand. In addition, you must develop research hypotheses on key targeting variables, usage occasions, and competitor brand awareness and associations, and any other key knowledge gaps that need to be addressed.

Your deliverables from this step include:

~ A detailed strategic hypothesis-testing brief document that outlines all hypotheses

~ A ready-to-field, quantitative testing design and survey questionnaire for current and prospective customers

Step 4: Test, Optimize, and Validate Hypotheses

Despite how well informed your strategy and positioning alternatives may be, you still must consider them to be only hypotheses—tentative assumptions made in order to draw out and test their logical or empirical consequences. In this step you will map out and project the potential power of each hypothesis and identify ways to make them even stronger. You accomplish this through quantitative testing with your target customers. You must use quantitative testing because these strategic decisions are too important to be left to judgment alone, and they are the basis for finalizing the brand positioning and architecture.

At this point, you may choose to select a research supplier to field your customer surveys, tabulate the data, and execute analytical methodologies that may include the following:

~ Stated versus derived benefit importance
~ Likely purchaser profiling
~ Demand-based segmentation
~ Purchase intent progression

Deliverables from this step should include:

~ Detailed electronic tables that summarize all data gathered
~ Presentation and summary document to detail all key findings and implications

Step 5: Create Brand Positioning and Architecture

With data in hand from the quantitative study, you are ready to build a strategic positioning statement and the architecture for your brand. The brand architecture is a detailed schematic diagram of how the key benefits and attributes of a brand work together to convey the overall positioning. The detailed architecture you develop for your brand will provide the strategic road map needed to successfully market it to customers and act as a yardstick against which all marketing and sales activities should be measured and aligned.

Your deliverables from this step include the following:

~ Final customer targeting recommendations
~ Brand positioning statement
~ Brand architectures (see examples shown in this chapter)

3

PLUG MARKETING INTO
THE ENTERPRISE

As you can see, brands stand at the center of your marketing enterprise, driving all your marketing efforts. So the question is, how do you make that brand the most effective engine it can be? Good question.

Developing an architecture for your brand is really the only place to start. Understanding your customer—and, sometimes, your customer's customer—provides the foundation that underlies every other scientific principle mentioned here. Without a brand architecture, you don't have a prayer of success; you literally *cannot* know how to focus all of your efforts without it.

In some cases, it's even more valuable to know what *not* to do.

To practice enterprise marketing management, it's important not just to do your homework in developing your brand architecture. You also have to reconfigure your thinking about how marketing should work with the *rest* of your company—sales, finance, operations, service, HR, and so forth—to apply this brand architecture. Furthermore, you should consider how marketing information flows from marketing to other departments and back again. Two key principles underlie this entire reconfiguration:

1. The benefits described in the brand architecture are simply too important to remain exclusively within the marketing department. They have to be shared with the rest of the company.
2. Marketing has to rely on the rest of the company to help it deliver the brand benefits and also to monitor what works and what doesn't. It's critical that marketing be plugged in to the information flow from all areas of the company.

The problem today is that marketing is an island, often both literally and figuratively shut off from the rest of the enterprise. While the rest of the enterprise has participated in an information revolution, granting most corporate branches access to critical information, marketing has stood on the sidelines. (See Figure 3.1.)

Since the early 1990s, this information revolution has manifested itself in far more forms than just new versions of Microsoft

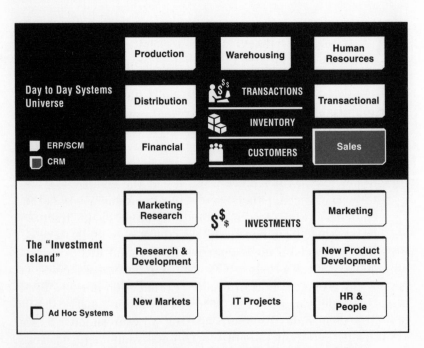

FIGURE 3.1   Marketing Is an Island in the Enterprise

Windows or the switch from, say, Lotus 1-2-3 to Microsoft Excel. Companies have implemented enterprise resource planning (ERP) systems, designed to solve the problem of islands of transaction and inventory information. This is precisely the problem that a company scrambles to solve when someone calls with that dreaded question: "Where's my order?"

Certainly, a customer service rep will have some answer to this question, but the real issue is whether it's a *correct* answer. Before the age of ERP, many large companies tracked inventory in several systems—a warehousing system, a finance system, and maybe even the ordering system. IT departments were forever trying to reconcile all the little packets and pools of information, the very definition of a Sisyphean task. Needless to say, they rarely ever got it right.

Solving the "islands of information" problem means that companies no longer sift through multiple systems, each with its own data. ERP systems create a single, primary data source shared among finance, warehousing, and ordering. Presto!—problem solved . . . at least for those concerned only about transaction and inventory information.

While ERP systems are useful, they don't provide information about the supply chain that is necessary to manage an increasingly complex network of buyers and suppliers. Companies needed programs that could look through the supply chain, programs that permitted greater integration and visibility of the location of products in their long journey from raw material to finished inventory. To do so, they looked to firms such as i2, which were developing supply chain management (SCM) software.

These forward-thinking companies understood that it was not enough just to track inventory when it's at the company's warehouse. True supply chain management involves keeping a tight rein on inventory as it works its way through the supply chain, gradually being transformed from raw material to finished product.

With supply chain management software and ERP software, companies could tell a customer exactly what portion of their order was in the warehouse, in transit, on the production line, or in raw form. Developing an answer to "Where's my order?" has gradually expanded to include the ability to look at your supplier's own inventory to determine whether additional manufacturing runs are scheduled—or even possible.

Even with such advancements, there still remained some other critical information trapped in islands throughout the company: customer data.

While it may be a relief, from a customer service standpoint, to be able to answer the "Where's my order?" question correctly every time, the bar should be set higher. If every customer touch point (service reps, web sites, direct sales, and retail) knew enough about each customer to use ERP/SCM-based information to sell more product, imagine the revenues that could result. The customer contact is already there; now the deal needs to be offered.

For example, if a customer calls in and asks, "Where's my order?," company information systems should snap into action. Call reps need to know information about the order, of course, but they should also know about the customer's buying history, delivery preferences, and product desires in order to deliver superior customer service. In addition, every rep must know about all of the company's interactions with each customer. If the customer had ordered from a different division or prefers to purchase products via a customer extranet, the company must make all these options possible in order to give the best possible service.

However, simply delivering quality service is never enough. The golden rule for any IT investment, as any chief information officer (CIO) will tell you, is that it's impossible to rationalize large investments in software unless you achieve at least one of the following:

~ Substantial increase in revenue
~ Dramatic reduction in operating costs
~ Dramatic reduction in capital employed (e.g., inventory on hand)

To date, the investments in ERP and SCM systems have pulled their weight by reducing operating costs and capital employed. They've turned IT and finance departments upside down, while whittling down the balance sheet significantly.

The integration of transaction and inventory information with the detailed, accurate profiles of customers has proven a powerful combination for both sales and customer service, as sales and service reps now have at their fingertips comprehensive and consistent information about their customers. The major developers of these total-solution CRM systems include players like Siebel Systems and

Oracle Corporation. These systems, which are still growing in acceptance and implementation, are expected to be the primary technology investment for companies for several years to come.

These days, most marketers have at least a passing familiarity with CRM systems. While this integration of customer data has driven results primarily through *sales force automation*—applying common selling processes to a common database of customer information—marketers are only now beginning to pay attention to its possibilities.

To this point, CRM has caused consternation among upper management, since it doesn't seem to be delivering the returns its users had expected. Any Luddite could tell you the reason why: You can invest in systems upon systems, but there's no guarantee you'll sell any more stuff.

The reason for this is simple—marketing hasn't been added to the CRM mix. CRM also means "can't replace marketing"—all of the best intentions to help a company cross-sell, or upsell, or just sell differently cannot happen unless marketing participates in the effort.

And the time for that to happen is now. Now is the chance for marketing to ride to the rescue. Now is the time to plug marketing in to these enterprise information sources, helping your company sell more, more profitably. The information revolution has taken place around marketers while they've stood in the eye of the hurricane. Now is the time for marketing to take up its own cause in the information revolution and put all of these investments to work.

Marketers know better than anyone that the highest accomplishments aren't measured in bits and bytes. No company ever shrank itself to greatness. The heart of all success lies in selling. Your company's ability to survive may very well depend on your ability to learn how to put these new information systems—and the information that flows through them—to work for you.

Nervous yet? Don't be. Although all this sounds complicated, it's not . . . as long as you're willing to put in a little effort. While there are many options for plugging marketing in to your enterprise, two areas of focus will drive the most immediate returns:

~ Connect marketing to sales.
~ Connect marketing to finance.

The focus you choose depends on the nature of your business. Companies that rely on direct selling with a sales force should focus on bringing sales and marketing together. Companies that sell to consumers through a third party may consider focusing on the upstream community first, integrating marketing with finance to better track the ROI of marketing investments. The choice is yours—but you must make a choice yourself, or your competitors will make it for you.

CONNECTING MARKETING TO SALES

Once marketing has developed the brand architecture, identifying the brand's compelling value proposition, a natural next step is to consider how to enable sales to communicate these benefits accurately. Because the brand architecture—and its shorthand version, the brand positioning—has been developed specifically to drive customer purchase intent, it should seem obvious for marketing to arm sales with this knowledge.

Unfortunately, as you probably already know, marketing and sales traditionally mix about as well as oil and water. The sales force often gets disappointed in marketing, since sales believes marketing creates campaigns and new products without any regard for customer needs.

Marketing, for its part, is often organized around products rather than markets or specific customer sets. Supplying sales forces with product-specific information, marketing expects the sales force to reconcile this information with the solution-oriented needs of their customers.

In short, an enormous amount of time and effort gets wasted. The inability of marketing to connect with sales offers a great opportunity for marketers who are plugged in to the sales information flow to sell more. In enterprise marketing management, marketers must feed the sales information flow that extends naturally to every customer, across every customer touch point. This information flow is created with the customer in mind, and it must be developed with a holistic perspective as well.

Marketers complain frequently about sales. They claim that sales forces can't execute well, focusing on quotas at the expense of learning about the product/service offering. And if sales doesn't provide feedback, marketing must rely on third parties and research firms to get the same information sales has in front of it every day.

There's also the matter of temperament. Many marketers think that selling is too much of a hands-on business, preferring to remain in the realm of concepts or advertising. Some marketers prefer the theoretical aspects of the product creation process, while others may just want to avoid the strict accountability that comes with sales.

Unfortunately, the disconnect between marketing and sales means that most selling content created by marketing either does not get used in the field or does not produce a tangible impact on revenue-generating activities. In fact, recent surveys of field sales reps at some of the largest and most respected companies indicate that upward of 90 percent of the material never even gets touched by sales. The main reasons cited are that "It doesn't conform to the way I sell" and "It's not relevant to the conversation I'm having with customers."

This means that nearly all the time and money spent on generating messaging content for the sales-customer interaction is for nothing, resulting in thousands or even millions of dollars of wasted effort each year. With every dollar wasted, the gap between marketing and sales grows larger, and the risk grows that marketing will be cut out of sales operations entirely.

Is this the case at your company? Ask yourself these two questions:

~ *Is my messaging sales-ready?* In other words, does it conform to the way salespeople sell? Is it organized so they can easily find the right content at the right time, based on the needs of the customers and sales force? Can it be composed into a format that is deliverable—easily and consistently—to each rep in every channel, in accordance with their existing training?

~ *Is my messaging customer-relevant?* That is, does it represent the conversation already taking place with customers? Have you aligned messaging in response to customer goals, requirements, and business needs—instead of product feature functionality—and provided corresponding supporting evidence? Is it formatted in a way that is useful to customers?

If you answer no to any of these questions and you want to see an example of how to better connect marketing to sales, read the American Express case study later in this chapter.

CONNECTING MARKETING TO FINANCE

So now you see how marketing can work with its downstream colleagues. Just as it's difficult to bring about a marriage between two such disparate partners, marketing also doesn't have the information to look back upstream—to apply financial discipline to its work. How can marketing possibly learn what drives sales—and what doesn't—if it's not able to track each investment and analyze the relevant sales? Marketing must strike an alliance with finance in order to track such revenues.

Plugging marketing into the finance function, in this instance, refers to the need for marketing to apply a rigorous, systematic approach to all of its spending. Enterprise marketing management requires an analytical approach, much like managing investments.

Knowing the specific results of marketing efforts allows marketers to correct their course along the way. The old practice of rolling the dice at the start of the year and measuring the results at the end of the year is over. You need to bring analytical financial rigor to your marketing investments, by connecting marketing to finance.

What form might this connection take? Considering that most financial systems are now part of ERP systems, this connection can be as simple as performing regular analyses of return on marketing spending. Or it can be as complex as an integration of marketing's planning, budgeting, and investing efforts with financial systems, so that real-time data snapshots are always available. Just as you manage your stock portfolio, you should manage your portfolio of marketing investments. Few companies have this capability in place, but it's only a matter of time. The sooner you make this connection between marketing and finance, the sooner you can tell the good marketing investments from the bad ones—and start putting your investments to good use.

CONNECTING MARKETING TO HUMAN RESOURCES

It's easy enough to grasp the necessary connections between marketing and the sales and financial departments. But what on earth could marketing and human resources (HR) have in common? It's simple: In the modern enterprise, the most valuable assets walk out the door every day. More important, they've got to be attracted enough to come through the door in the first place.

Marketing develops a brand architecture that is intended to drive customer purchase intent. But what about driving employee work intent? That may sound like an absurd iteration of the problem, but the savviest employers realize that the winners of the game are the ones with the strongest team members. As a marketer, connecting to HR means helping HR determine the best players to communicate your message. How do you attract the sales superstar? The next logistics wizard who will save your company millions? The R&D specialist who will put your company on the map with a groundbreaking product?

Marketing must translate the power of its brand to potential employees. Otherwise, hiring becomes just a shot in the dark, and you may not get a second chance at that make-or-break employee.

The role of enterprise marketing management in this instance is simply to develop a brand architecture for attracting employees, just as you would develop a brand architecture for driving purchase intent. See Chapter 2, to think through the scientific method from an employee's perspective. The same tools that work for attracting, selling to, and retaining customers can be applied to attracting employees.

The real shame is that marketing and HR rarely come together in the best interest of the company. Applying marketing talent to attracting employees results for the most part from serendipity. CEOs would be wise to not get caught up in traditional silos and consider how marketing skills can be used in new ways. All of the customer marketing in the world might not make a difference if your employees aren't up to the task of delivering what's been sold.

CONNECTING MARKETING TO OPERATIONS

The brand holds sway over the entire organization, and operations is no exception. Even the smallest operational details can take on enormous importance when magnified across the entire enterprise. Every part of the organization interacts and communicates with your customers, so it behooves every marketer to think about every potential customer touch point.

The term *operations* doesn't really do justice to the breadth of capabilities required. On a simpler basis, if sales and marketing represent demand generation, operations stands for demand fulfillment. It's every single event related to delivering on the promise of the brand, once the customer has made a purchase.

While marketers may wax eloquently about customer lifetime value, it's really up to operations to make sure it happens.

Ergo, if marketing doesn't connect to operations, this can't happen. Operations, in this context, refers to manufacturing, service, support, warehousing, delivery, maintenance, and other activities. Operations is critical to creating and maintaining a brand experience, the subject of Chapter 4.

CASE STUDY: American Express

CONNECTING MARKETING TO SALES
TO DRIVE INCREASED CARD ACCEPTANCE

American Express has recognized the importance of connecting marketing to merchants, most specifically through the concept of *customer message management* (CMM).

The company found general across-the-board agreement on the importance of consistent brand messaging, but had trouble executing the concept. Coordinating all of the messages being delivered across all channels may sound like a good idea, but making it happen—ensuring a consistent message at the call center or web site or when a salesperson has a face-to-face meeting with customers—is no easy feat.

The company faced several challenges:

- The sales force reported back to marketing that they were suffering from information overload.
- The company needed to balance the quantity of product information with the specific needs of customers or customer segments
- The skill sets of sales reps varied across the company— meaning that some were able to synthesize all of the marketing information, while many were not.

- National team and larger accounts benefited from more experienced sales reps and accordingly were able to craft the information overload into consistent selling messages with customer-specific adjustments.
- Small- to middle-market sales reps, with more accounts to cover but in many instances possessing less experience, struggled to deliver the right brand benefits to their accounts so as to communicate the value of the American Express relationship.

Over the course of a year and a half, the company sought to hire about 100 to 150 new sales reps, focusing on that smaller to mid-range opportunity. Obviously, one concern was that these people came with their own baggage from their previous careers, and it takes a long time to instill new thinking within a salesperson.

Another concern was inconsistent message delivery. Several years ago, American Express performed an audit of the materials that salespeople presented to customers, and found there was little differentiation. The company determined that it needed to understand customers' specific needs and integrate those with the messages that American Express is delivering. The company had spent considerable money, time, and resources training salespeople to sell based on the needs of customers. It had spent significant labor-hours investing in those resources. The problem was that all of the strategies that marketing was creating did not necessarily strengthen the message.

In the small to middle market, sales cycles are becoming significantly more complex, looking more like sales cycles of a national team. So salespeople who typically would go in and sell an account in one or two visits are now looking at an extended sales cycle, since they are working with more educated customers who may actually know more about the industry than the salespeople. So the company needed to create a method by which these salespeople could become more educated. At the same time, all salespeople are driven to make quotas, which tend to increase every year, a factor the company needed to take into account.

All of these external pressures and the information overload ultimately lead to disjointed messaging. So the company decided to determine a way to bridge this messaging gap through a collaborative partnership between sales and marketing.

American Express decided to take a lesson from the success of others. The company laid out, in partnership with a group called the Sales Executive Council, some of the best-in-class procedures that other companies with similar challenges had used. The company grouped these strategies into three primary areas: freeing up rep time, increasing rep effectiveness, and reorganizing efforts around the customers.

The company also created a sales intelligence center, where any data needed throughout the sales process is housed in one place and a team of cross-functional individuals can tackle any business issue.

Anytime a company tries to alter its operations, there is a significant challenge in preparing people for change. The company definitely had some adoption challenges, but tried to address those by proactively approaching the sales teams in developing the collaborative environment.

American Express formed a steering committee of end users to discuss the issue of customer messaging and how that could best be executed. These people were established sales leaders, perceived as thought leadership, and their mantra was to confirm, condense, and convince others in the organization so that once the company agreed upon a solution, that would be the path that would be embraced by the sales teams.

The Solution

Ultimately, American Express launched an initiative called Sales Force Online. It has been so successful that account managers are working to find access to the same information. The company is now in the process of expanding the application to create a more holistic view of the customer relationship.

As a result, American Express has leveraged the initiative as a key communication portal. American Express can adjust the value proposition in conjunction with sales and deliver nuances to it quickly at a centrally managed content location.

At any given time, American Express has an estimated 300 to 500 different marketing programs with which a salesperson has to be adept to sell to a prospect. So the company created a filter through which sales reps could create, based on the needs and objectives of that customer, an appropriate marketing solution, then print out an agreement and all of the marketing materials they would need.

One of the key areas of the information portal is called Roadmap, which American Express developed in partnership with Ventaso, a leading provider of customer message management solutions. Roadmap takes all of the elements that a salesperson uses throughout the sales cycle—the value information, customer testimonials, and survey findings—and loads them into a central knowledge database. American Express wanted to leverage the good work already being done, but also marry the sales and marketing effectiveness and layer different product rollouts into one database.

So how did American Express get to the outputs and craft the appropriate message?

In cooperation with its partners at Ventaso, American Express surveyed its existing customer base to learn the benefits of accepting the American Express card from the perspective of the customer. Just getting the perspective wasn't enough because, as it turned out, marketing and sales interpreted customer perspectives differently. By working together, sales and marketing agreed on customer messaging that they could deliver in an automated fashion. In doing so, they managed to create a partnership between marketers and salespeople, defusing a traditionally adversarial relationship.

Now an American Express salesperson or an account manager can customize all of the documents and all communication points with a customer. The company has moved away from that boilerplated messaging and toward unique messaging based on the needs of a particular customer.

On the back end, the solution gives American Express incredible market intelligence. Within a particular market segment, the company can see what the salesperson delivered in the presentation and the features that resonated with this particular account. Then the company can determine in similar presentations what showed up 100 percent of the time and what showed up 50 percent of the time, which tells the company what is resonating in the marketplace.

American Express is in the nascent stages of leveraging this technology. The company is currently focusing on the direct sales challenge but is also looking to expand to the call center environments as well as an interface with its Internet application. And there is interest in global expansion and a rollout to other organizations within the company.

The technology has aided American Express in three key areas: reducing the cost of acquisition, improving sales rep productivity, and, most important, enhancing the quality of customer messaging. In terms of hard numbers, the pilot program engineered savings of $240,000 over the first six months—a significant sum when compounded across multiple regions around the world. Although it's too early to tell, initial results point to significant improvements in close rates and sales volume.

In order to provide sales reps with the most accurate and timely data, American Express now posts its marketing collateral online, rather than printing it and updating it via hard copy. The readiness and speed-to-market components of the program, as well as its central location, give salespeople the appropriate information, at the appropriate time, in the appropriate format.

Most important, however, American Express now knows that when salespeople go out to speak to prospects, they have worked in concert with marketing to create an effective, targeted message. Marketing can now manage content and deploy new messages rapidly. The continuous feedback loop also allows the sales force to let marketing and other reps know what's working and what isn't. Ineffective messages can be refined, refocused, and reintroduced to the marketplace in rapid order.

Sales Force Online has provided American Express with a wealth of information—so much so that account managers are seeking access to the same information. The company is now in the process of expanding the application in order to have a more holistic view of the customer relationship.

Founding Principles: American Express Customer Message Management

- **Customer relevant.** Messaging should be based on customer-centric issues (business goals, needs, and requirements), not product-centric features.
- **Sales ready.** Messaging should conform to the way salespeople have been trained to sell (needs determination and value alignment).
- **Effective structure.** Messaging should be structured in a consistent, reusable, template-based approach that can be deployed across a company for more efficient content creation and management.
- **Real-time access.** Messaging should be available and delivered online to the right person, at the right time, using a

simple, intuitive user interface designed to replicate the sales and customer communication process.

- **Personalized outputs.**   Messaging should be presentable in customized outputs based on specified needs, so that customer communications reflect the unique business goals and requirements expressed in each sales opportunity.
- **Continuous improvement.**   Messaging should be managed and updated based on proactive, interactive analysis and feedback to ensure maximum impact and field effectiveness.

MARKETER'S SCIENTIFIC METHOD: PLUG MARKETING INTO THE ENTERPRISE

How specifically do you plug marketing into the enterprise? The procedure breaks down into two stages: promoting the brand's benefits and integrating marketing into the overall enterprise.

> *Marketing must evangelize the benefits of the brand.*

Step 1: Evaluate and Address How Your Brand(s) Positioning Has Been Communicated and Engaged Throughout the Company

~ Does the sales force have a clear understanding of the benefits that drive customer purchase intent, or are they perhaps the reason why every customer conversation comes down to price—sales reps don't really know what to say?

~ Does marketing focus on products, while sales has to sell solutions? Have your communication efforts been designed for the customer—and for all of the different situations that your sales force might encounter with your customers?

~ Does marketing actually *listen* when sales says what it needs to drive customer purchase?

~ Do you know how much of marketing's efforts is actually *used* by sales, rather than simply discarded?

~ Are you measuring the ROI of marketing investments?

~ Does your company know what benefits HR should communicate to attract and retain the best talent?

~ Do you feel constrained by your company's industry, location, reputation? Do good candidates just not want to work here?

~ Are your recruiting efforts time consuming, ridiculously expensive, and sometimes fraught with error? Are you not attracting the right people?

~ Are your HR marketing efforts little more than blasé job descriptions based on boilerplate?

~ Do you wonder why your competitors seem to be able to attract better talent?

~ Have you discovered that you can't get the best candidates by simply paying more?

> ***Marketing must be integrated into the company
> information flow.***

Step 2: Evaluate Marketing's Integration with and Participation in Developing Information Systems

~ Is marketing participating in efforts to launch CRM capabilities?

~ Does marketing participate in determining how ERP- or CRM-based information will be provided to customers?

~ Has marketing connected with finance to develop an investment-driven approach—connecting marketing investment with specific sales returns?

Marketing hasn't traditionally played a role in determining where to make investments in information technology. Wake up! It's the twenty-first century! Information technology—and, most important, the information flow that it creates—is a critical element of strategically differentiating one brand from another. If one of your brand benefits involves service, how are information technology investments delivering on that needed benefit? Marketers can't be content sitting back and hoping that the company is able to deliver on the desired brand benefits. They have to jump into the fray.

For that reason, marketers must assume greater responsibility for all information technology investments. To be blunt, nearly every investment that information technology makes can be made to evangelize the brand (supporting sales or service interactions with customers), deliver on the brand positioning (perhaps providing information about where your product is *before* it shows up at your loading dock, to deliver on the brand benefit of easy to do business with), and ultimately track the results of marketing investments.

Every piece of information generated by your company is important to marketers. The only way for marketing to connect to the enterprise is to seize every opportunity to drive information technology investments.

Sitting on the sidelines won't work anymore. Just as marketers must consult on discussions over whether the company needs another manufacturing plant, they must likewise consult on whether that next investment in information technology will help deliver on the brand positioning or give marketers greater ability to manage marketing investments. Nothing is more important to your company.

PART II

Manage Your Brand, Not Your Customer

4

TAKE OWNERSHIP
OF THE BRAND EXPERIENCE

Once you've brought marketing into the company fold, what's next? The opportunities are myriad. Making a conscious effort to connect marketing to the rest of the company will help you achieve two important objectives. First, you can help spread the power and knowledge of what drives purchase intent for the brand across the rest of the company. Thus, even when the delivery truck driver shows up at your customer's door, he or she knows how your company's brand differs from (and, of course, stands above!) that of your competitors.

Second, and on a broader scale, by connecting marketing to the information flow of the enterprise, you put marketing in a much better position to drive value for customers. You can constantly learn and evaluate which marketing investments are paying off and which ones are not.

It's important for marketing to participate in the decision making surrounding information technology investments. But while marketing may not have the technological savvy to add value in comparing technology investments, the key is that the technology itself is not important; the customer is.

Unfortunately, marketing and information technology tend to be the Hatfields and McCoys of the enterprise, seeing eye to eye only long enough to stare one another down. Marketing profession-als are reluctant to embrace technology and, as a result, frequently abdicate their role as caretakers of the brand experience.

Don't believe us? Take this simple quiz. Which do you consider to be more important for your company:

~ Providing your customer's engineers access to up-to-date product specifications or providing the customer's purchasing department access to an invoice history?
~ Investing in a new CRM system to improve customer service's ability to recognize customers and potentially cross-sell or creating a product marketplace?
~ Developing a product comparison tool to help self-service customers or investing in outbound teleselling capabilities?

The answers are . . . there are no answers. These are trick questions. In truth, it's impossible to know the answers until marketing asserts its role as the *owner of the brand experience* and evaluates its information- or service-oriented investments on the basis of one primary criterion: the ability to help the company sell more products and services.

Every single one of the theoretical investments described here has its merits; in the abstract, none is better than any of the others. But all of them have something in common: a definite, measurable impact on the brand experience.

But just what *is* this brand experience, and how is it different from the brand architecture and its shorthand cousin, the brand positioning?

The brand experience is simply a way to describe the sum of a customer's interactions with a brand. If a brand is the bundle of functional and emotional benefits, attributes, icons, and symbols that, in total, constitutes the meaning of a product or service, then the brand experience is the name for a customer's complete experience with the brand. The term *brand* implies a perspective from the company outward (inside out). The term *brand experience* implies a perspective from the customer to every interaction with the company (outside in). As you might imagine, customer interactions aren't limited to simply making decisions regarding one product as opposed to another. The brand experience would include the customer's actual experience with the product, as well as every other aspect of interaction with your company. For everyday consumer products, this would include how the product is merchandised in the store, the dynamics of the product itself, learning how to set up the product (i.e., negotiating the user's manual), the experience of using the product (whether that's pouring a bowl of cereal or using a new toaster), and even the experience of getting repair.

Every single step in a customer's relationship with your company goes into forming aspects of the brand experience (see Figure 4.1). While the elements may differ, the brand experience for a more industrial product is arguably even more important. As the product or service complexity/risk increases, the value that the customer places on the overall experience becomes even more important.

As you might imagine, the brand experience covers a lot of ground. As a result, every company struggles with how to optimize it. There are plenty of blind alleys you could head down in search of this optimization, but in truth, the best answer already exists right in front of you.

Take a close look at Figure 4.1. A brand experience is defined by how your customers purchase and use your products or services, not by how your company is organized. Despite the best efforts of

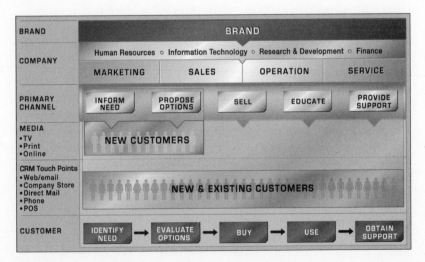

FIGURE 4.1   Defining the Brand Experience

companies to reengineer the way they interact with their customers, they're still constrained by departmental silos that hinder the ability to deliver customer satisfaction (and, of course, drive profitable sales higher and higher).

Marketing must take ownership of this brand experience framework, and ownership starts with a prioritization of the use of customer information. In short, marketing must participate in and drive decisions, which requires a trade-off of time and resources to deliver appropriate information at any step along the way.

For example, why should customers purchase a jet engine from your company if they're not confident in your ability to provide service? For most industrial companies, the value of the brand experience far exceeds the value of the product sold. If Alcoa sells Ford Motor Company aluminum to make its new SUV, of course the aluminum is important. However, it's important within a context. If the Ford engineers aren't able to machine the aluminum properly, or if the aluminum doesn't show up at the right production plant at the right time, or if the invoicing for the aluminum isn't correct, the brand experience suffers. Quality information about the product— say, the delivery schedule—can be more valuable than the product itself, especially if it is has an impact on the ability to complete a production schedule worth millions.

When the brand experience encompasses all elements of a company-customer connection, the truth becomes obvious: Marketers have only been playing in part of the overall marketing game. With enterprise marketing management, marketers must leave their traditional territory and venture out to take responsibility for a lot more.

The brand architecture gives you a framework of brand benefits to apply. In addition, by preaching the benefits across the enterprise, you will make the entire company your army, mobilized and ready to communicate and deliver on these benefits.

Finally, when it steps up to the plate and takes a more significant role in information technology investments, marketing will be well placed to drive IT to track and build the brand experience over time.

The brand experience has several different components. The first two elements are the most important: your brand and your customer. If you are missing either of these, then you're, no doubt, in trouble. The brand is at the top of the hierarchy because that's what marketers are supposed to keep central. Note that it's not just something that sits at marketing's table. As stated earlier, the brand *is* the business. But the experience is built entirely around the customer. It's worth repeating that the way your company is organized—who's in sales, who's in marketing, or who's in operations—is completely irrelevant to your customers. They simply don't and won't ever care—nor should they.

Nearly everyone has experienced customer frustration when someone from a company with which you're doing business says something like, "That's not my department" or "That's Accounting, I'm in Sales." It happens every day—and, though you may not like to admit it, it probably happens in your company.

Building upward from the customer, the next element of the brand experience is customer touch points. These are just what they sound like—every potential place where you might interact with your customer. Some examples would be retail stores, call centers, web sites, warehouses, direct sales encounters (person to person), and e-mail. Customer touch points represent a direct connection between you and your customers without the interaction of a third party. The term *customer touch point* further connotes a degree of interactivity not found in traditional media.

The next element of the brand experience is the traditional media with which most marketers are already very comfortable (print ads, TV ads, promotions). While customer touch points are highly interactive and potentially relevant across every element of the brand experience, these traditional media concentrate on bringing in new customers—or, at least, reminding existing customers why they need to buy again. The focus is on the demand generation side of the table. Except in very rare circumstances, these media are simply too expensive to be employed in helping customers actually obtain or use follow-up service for their purchase. New media represent an opportunity, which will be discussed later.

The next element has special significance. It's the primary channel and the steps that you take as a company to match up with a specific customer. This is the yin that you bring to your customer's yang, your salt to their pepper. The primary channel represents the dominant vehicle for serving your customer across all elements of the brand experience. The primary channel serves as a reminder that you have a choice in determining how you would like to serve your customers and that your channel decisions should be backed up by a specific strategy. Too many companies wear their channels like a straightjacket, never daring to ask their customers how they would like to be served—or even whether they'd prefer to serve themselves. (Think about the self-scan checkout lane at the grocery store, immensely popular ever since its debut.) It only took grocery stores 10 years to figure this out.

The final element in the brand experience is your internal organization—departments, functions, and silos that are already in place. How well they fit into the overall picture isn't just dependent on marketing, but marketing should have a say in retrofitting them if necessary.

Now that you have a better idea of the moving parts of a brand experience, let's take a closer look at these core elements and explore customer interactions with each to ensure that you have a clear picture of the task ahead.

IDENTIFY NEED (INFORM NEED)

The first task in determining the parameters of the brand experience is to *identify need*. This step begins before a customer has had any interaction with your company, at the moment when a customer determines that he or she has a particular need for a product or service. In the strictest sense, this customer recognizes this need and potentially also understands that a product or service exists to fulfill it.

This is the domain in which marketers would traditionally say that they "build awareness." However, awareness alone is almost never enough to actually motivate a customer to move forward. Enterprises have spent millions of dollars building awareness that never actually turned into a purchase. Customers knowing that your brand exists is no guarantee that they believe it will deliver the specific benefits to fulfill their needs.

Scientific marketers use advertising and communication media not just to build awareness, but to highlight how their brand delivers the benefits to fulfill customer needs. It's the difference between a hot dog vendor simply saying, "I'm here," and the same vendor enticing you by saying, "How about something delicious and convenient for lunch today?"

On a more subtle level, the brand benefit communications process also works in reverse. Brand communications can actually *teach* a customer that a need exists—and then highlight how the brand delivers the benefits that satisfy the need. Think about products that you might have at your home or office that didn't even exist 20 years ago, such as PDAs, cell phones, or even personal computers. Buyers of personal computers had to be taught the need first, then instructed about why a specific brand would deliver the range of benefits to meet that need.

Marketers must think about how to add value to the brand experience in the *identify need (inform need)* stage in the following ways:

- ~ By developing robust brand architecture and communicating emotional and functional benefits
- ~ By integrating with the customer's supply chain to make reordering or need identification automatic
- ~ By providing partner-oriented selling information to put the broader partner network (distributors, alliance partners) to work

Historically, helping customers identify a need has been the domain of sales and marketing. For most companies, marketing actually *stops* after this stage, handing off responsibility for what happens next to other functions in the company.

And therein lies the problem. Constant handoffs from function to function and department to department don't take into account the importance of a holistic view of the brand experience—and the fact that providing information is critical to differentiating *any* company's offering.

EVALUATE OPTIONS (PROPOSE OPTIONS)

Once a customer has identified his or her needs, it's now up to you to decide how to close that deal. You need to move to the second element in the brand experience as your potential customer begins to *evaluate options*.

When the brand awareness efforts take hold, a customer will say, "Yes, I have a need" (which could also mean "Yes, my company has a need," or even "Yes, my family has a need"). Thanks to either spontaneity or the assistance of your tireless marketing communication efforts, the customer now moves to the stage of evaluating options.

Ideally, your marketing efforts have been so persuasive that this stage is perfunctory: What options are there other than your own? But for many companies, this point is the critical stage, in which the customer determines a set of potential solutions and then evaluates each of those solutions against the personal need. This is also the stage in which your brand positioning efforts come to fruition.

In the best-case scenario, you've developed a brand positioning that helps your customer understand how your product delivers the benefits that perfectly meet the customer's needs—and also why your competitors' products are not the right ones. This evaluation can be as simple as comparing the nutrition information on two boxes of cookies to determine which has the lowest fat content. On a more emotional level, it might come down to the fact that one brand of cookies reminds customers of good times in their own childhood, and they want their children to enjoy that experience as well.

On a more complex scale, for a product such as a fleet of trucks or jumbo jets, the evaluation stage might last for months and require a detailed analysis of functionality, price, difficulty of integration, numerous interviews of signature clients, and excruciatingly complex negotiations.

At this point, the customer makes up his or her mind and decides what to buy. As anyone who is in the business of selling expensive products and services can testify, this stage can be absolute agony for the enterprise. The temptation is always present to take a shortcut to success—chopping prices to make a quick buck, for instance.

Don't give in to temptation. When making investments in understanding or impacting this element of the brand experience, don't get blinded by cost reduction at the expense of differentiation. This stage is also where the question of pricing will enter the game. Generally speaking, the greater the importance of price competition, the less actual marketing is going on.

Price is what all buyers fall back on in the absence of any other available benefits. If a company promotes a product or service without demonstrating the benefits that drive purchase intent, the buyer has little choice but to make a decision based on price. If you don't give your customer some other basis on which to make a decision, rest assured he or she will make price a big part of the process.

Whether you're selling plastics or pierogies, delivering specific brand benefits gives your customer something to consider beyond price. Articulating and delivering these benefits is what marketing is really all about.

In what ways might a marketer consider adding value to the brand experience in the *evaluate options (propose options)* stage?

~ By continuing to communicate your differentiating brand benefits, based on your brand architecture.

~ By compiling and providing detailed comparative purchase information *with* your product and service information. Do the analysis and comparison on your customer's behalf, remembering to position your competitors for your benefit where possible.

~ By providing product and service configuration tools that may let him/her choose or configure from multiple suppliers.

~ By providing expansive recommendation options driven by past purchase history (e.g., Amazon's referral links to similar or related products or services). In other words, use what you know about your customer's past behavior to recommend products or configurations that only you could know.

~ By providing interactive profiling tools to identify and choose the correct product or service.

~ By driving outbound selling scripts based on historical purchase data combined with detailed customer information.

~ By building upselling or cross-selling capability for salespeople to help customers understand what products or services are naturally purchased together or might be combined to deliver a unique capability or fill a unique need.

BUY (SELL)

The purchase is the coup de grâce, the moment around which this entire process—and, indeed, the entire economy—revolves. Of course, this act varies from swinging through the checkout lane to determining a detailed delivery schedule to locations around the world. This element of the brand experience includes all of the details of the delivery, including pricing, timing, and recipients. The purchase can take moments, or it can take years.

Purchasing is another venue where information and process technology have altered the way the customer does business. In the just-in-time inventory management system embraced by many manufacturing-intensive industries, information about the arrival of the product and its usage might be more important than the product itself. For a large manufacturer such as Toyota, the value of a nondelivered part may only be a few hundred dollars, but the cost of a work stoppage can quickly grow into the millions.

This element of the brand experience has seen feverish activity in recent years as companies embrace Web-based transactions and improve customer access to information. In most instances, these efforts have focused on taking information that already resides in ERP systems (traditional finance, purchasing, distribution, ware-housing, etc.) and providing it to customers. This could come in a form as simple as giving customers access to their invoices online, or it could take on more complex dimensions.

Marketing needs to think about how it can use the purchase itself and all of the information around it to differentiate the company and its brands. Anyone can imagine how much less expensive it might be to force customers to go to a web site to enter information or execute a transaction. The question is, however, is that what your customers want? Does it build value for your customers, taken in the context of the total brand experience?

Many companies have stumbled in their zeal to move customer interactions online. Companies have labored for years and spent millions of dollars to try to give their customers access to all sorts of data. However, in many cases, these companies have seen little or no return. They haven't stopped to answer simple questions such as the following:

~ How does this information create value and differentiate our company in the eyes of our customer?
~ Does every customer get everything that we offer, or do
  we have a way of differentiating the information we provide for our best customers, for our medium-best customers, and so on?

~ Is this a requirement of doing business or a way to make us stand above the crowd?
~ Is this more important than doing X (spending money on communication, traditional marketing, developing new products, or the like)?
~ What is the cost of providing this information, and where do we make this up? Do we charge for it?

It's worth noting that not all of this information and customer service effort needs to be provided to every customer for free. A key part of involving marketing in all aspects of the brand experience is to make certain that the company seizes on new revenue streams. For instance, companies can create different service levels based on customer profitability. Platinum customers get access to more information and opportunities than silver customers. Marketing must incorporate the power of information into differentiating its service and delivering value to its customers. Otherwise, the company is just keeping up with the Joneses, treading water rather than making headway.

In what ways might a marketer consider adding value to the brand experience in the *buy* (*sell*) stage?

~ By using the brand architecture to differentiate the purchase process and continuing to deliver the brand benefits that drive purchase intent
~ By considering how your brand benefits and, potentially, the character of your brand can be used to differentiate your offering from your competition
~ By recognizing your most important customers (as you define them) so that they know they're important—at this stage and at every stage of the brand experience
~ By integrating your sale so deeply into the customer's purchasing process that it becomes as automatic as breathing
~ By differentiating your offering to allow for cumulative purchase effects—in essence, giving better products/ services to the best customers, while improving margin overall (e.g., platinum customers receive premier pages, such as those offered by Dell Computer to its best customers)

USE (EDUCATE)

Congratulations! You've closed the deal, and the customer has purchased your product. For many marketing departments, this information shows up as dollars or pounds or cases, and the customer is forgotten. What's next? Now your customer must utilize your product or service once it's been delivered. If your product is, say, the chocolate chips that you supply to Nabisco to bake into Chips Ahoy! cookies, then the application would be baking the chips into the cookies for eventual packaging and shipment to grocery stores.

An inevitable part of offering a product or service any more complicated than a fast-food hamburger is the necessity of providing additional information or contact after the sale. And this is where most companies fumble the ball. Flush with the success of the sale, they lose sight of the fact that their job is *not* done just because the customer has signed on the dotted line. Aside from the obvious shortsightedness in failing to maintain customers, companies miss out on all sorts of opportunities to continue selling, upselling, cross-selling, and selling services.

There's also the matter of preserving and enhancing your reputation. Just because you sell a commodity product that forms one aspect of another product, are you confident that your customers know what to do with it on their line? Could you help customers improve their throughput using your product? Or, even better, could you sell them differentiated services that might drive your margins higher *and* leave your customers more satisfied with the overall brand experience?

There is likely an array of possibilities for you to help your customers in ways that you're not pursuing today but are uniquely capable of offering. If you're not doing so, you're leaving money on the table. Many of the world's finest companies have legions of engineers that are locked up in developing products. Unlocking that engineering resource in the form of *services* for customers should be considered by many companies.

An icon of American business, Jack Welch, former CEO of General Electric (the company of superbly engineered products such as jet engines, energy plants, and medical equipment, in addition to being owners of NBC, GE Capital, and a host of others), noted that GE is in the service business. Even in the case of GE's jet engine production, the majority of the profit from the sale of these engines comes *not* from the product itself but from the service contract that is sold with it.

Marketers have the skill sets necessary to develop new business models and think about how their companies could better manage the brand experience to drive profits. Who else is going to do it? Nobody else combines the awareness of customers' needs with the knowledge of the company's capabilities to accurately forecast and seize upon opportunities.

Marketing, the future is up to you.

Before we leave the domain of application and usage, we have to consider how to leverage information technology. As an example, think about how computer operating systems have changed. Both the new Windows XP and Mac OS X use the Internet to stay plugged in to Microsoft and Apple, respectively, to ensure that you're always using the most up-to-date version. In addition, both companies can use this electronic listening capability to conduct repair or identify the source of problems that you might have.

Why don't *your* products use this same capability to offer your customers frequent enhancements and automatic problem solving so as to improve your brand experience? Why make your customers have a less-than-perfect experience if they don't have to?

Marketing must understand enough about information technology to recognize what's possible. If it does not, then your company is just wishing and hoping that these sorts of opportunities will bubble to the surface. One way of ensuring that these opportunities arise and exist is to enforce the idea that marketing has ownership of the brand experience.

In what ways might a marketer consider adding value to the brand experience in the *use* (*educate*) stage?

- ~ By leveraging the framework of the brand architecture to continue to communicate brand benefits and position your brand
- ~ By providing just-in-time information about the application of the product
- ~ By incorporating with the product learning courses for its use

~ By developing and providing differentiated services to assist throughout the use of the product (e.g., call center or online access to engineers who are experienced users)

~ By helping customers find other customers who also use the product and could benefit from sharing experiences

~ By supporting and providing monitoring of your products to ensure that they are always in perfect condition

~ By providing ancillary, updated information that drives value for your product (e.g., Tivo provides the subscription service to TV listings that drives the value of the hardware)

OBTAIN SUPPORT (PROVIDE SUPPORT)

We're all familiar with the role of support—and, unfortunately, we're all familiar with support's failure to deliver on its promise. In this instance, service can also be referred to as *support*—once a customer has made a purchase and then applied that purchase, what often arises is the need for service. This function comprises everything from repair of broken purchases to upgrades of those operating at a lower-than-optimum level.

Here, we're referring to service from the customer's perspective. Service from the company's perspective is often quite different. For example, customer service reps may be working at a call center, but in fact actually reach across all of the customer stages. Customer services can help you configure a product (evaluating options) that you purchase elsewhere—as with a live Dell rep helping you configure a particular PC, which you then buy online. The same customer service rep could take your credit card for an order (purchase) or aid you in installing a new piece of hardware or software (application or usage). Finally, if after all this, your new computer doesn't work, you can call back and figure out where the problem lies. This is the form of service that will be the locus of this discussion.

For most companies, *support* as we've defined it is seen as something of a nuisance. As we mentioned in the example of companies dialing in to provide just-in-time service or maintenance, there are new ways of helping your customers avoid downtime altogether and, in so doing, building an even tighter bond with them, thereby improving your brand experience. What is the likelihood that a buyer of your product is going to change to a different one if you're constantly updating and improving it with new information? How about if you identify potential service issues even before your customers do?

Many companies now want to spend the least possible amount of time on support calls, hoping the problems will eventually just go away. Smart companies have figured out that contact with customers is where you actually stand the greatest chance of making more money by selling more stuff. When your customer support or customer service reps answer the phone, are they armed with everything they need to know about the brand in order to sell more?

Many companies are in the position of needing to sell service just to pay the bills. Auto dealers, for example, probably wouldn't cry too hard about losing the new car sales portion of their business. However, if you took away their service franchise, there would be no auto dealers left. Again, the product represents the means for creating the relationship, whereas the service is how you make money. If marketing doesn't own the brand experience as it relates to service, you're losing a great opportunity to differentiate yourself in the marketplace and generate higher margins. *Every* company is a service company, whether it likes it or not. Support is the area where you can build a sustainable competitive advantage—essentially, an unassailable brand experience that will lead to higher sales and higher margins.

When it comes to leveraging information technology in the support element of the brand experience, the opportunities are nearly overwhelming. Here's a simple question: Are your product manuals available online? Most companies' aren't. In these times, providing someone at an 800 number who is available only after a long wait and a frustrating navigation through a maze of menu options ("press 2 for service; press 3 for mailing address . . .") is just not enough.

Because most companies fail to see the value of support in the overall scheme of the brand experience, they shunt it off to people who know the *least* about the product. Why do so many companies connect you to a know-nothing customer service rep (especially when you may be their most valuable customer), when it's just as easy for you to send an e-mail or an instant message to someone who knows you and the products that you buy? Again, the information technology is available that would allow you to route your most important customers deep inside your company to get the support they deserve from a knowledgeable source, rather than routing your best (and most profitable customers) through a central system.

Providing differentiated service is where IT can help put your company at the top of the heap. If you're treating everyone the same, then you're not optimizing your brand experience, and you're vulnerable to displacement by a company that really understands what your customers want.

In what ways might a marketer consider adding value to the brand experience in the *obtain support* (*provide support*) stage?

- ~ By using your brand architecture as a guide to delivering the support-related benefits that you know drive customer purchase intent
- ~ By building intelligence into your products to inform you when they need service or repair
- ~ By giving your customers access to a product knowledge base
- ~ By delivering automatic product or service updates

TOO MUCH INFORMATION?

How should a company weigh the trade-offs that are inevitable when deciding among the numerous ways to enhance the brand experience?

The answer, of course, is marketing.

Once marketing assumes ownership of the entire brand experience, it must apply portfolio theory to any potential developments that might enhance the brand experience and determine which options will help sell more of what it has to offer. Sure, it might be nice to give your customers everything imaginable, but it only really makes sense if it is actually going to help you increase sales and margins. The science of marketing demands a great deal of analytical rigor when it comes to what you provide your customers and what you charge them for this.

Marketers must think outside of their traditional box to own everything that the company does to interact with its customers.

Marketers have to apply scientific principles in evaluating the trade-offs to determine which investments in the brand experience will earn a sufficient ROI and which investments should be avoided. Most marketers simply avoid the conversation altogether and stick to playing around with the advertising agency. Without their input, decisions of enormous portent, which determine what information might be communicated to customers, are taking place down the hall. In the age of information and service, marketing that focuses too much on such traditional venues as promotions and advertising is the equivalent of dinosaurs circling the tar pits. You—or your company—might not survive such an error.

Most marketing departments focus on the first element of the brand experience, leaving the rest to mere chance and the whims of the CIO. Unless marketing can step up and assume responsibility, there can be no substantive, meaningful, or long-lasting change in a company's operations—and the bottom line isn't going to improve. Realistically, what is the likelihood that the CIO, or any staff function for that matter, is going to develop a way to differentiate your current products or services with information—and, from there, figure out a way to leverage it into more revenue or closer relationships with customers?

To put it bluntly, marketing *deserves* ownership of the brand experience. Why? Because marketing can provide a better experience for both customer and company. Marketing understands what the company's customers need and want, and should learn to understand how the company can best meet—or generate—those needs. This doesn't mean that companies toss a bunch of undifferentiated offerings in the air and see which ones customers chase. Rather, marketing must pursue a targeted, focused strategy aimed at bringing maximum value to the maximum number of customers.

Of course, it would be nice to be able to offer everything to everyone, but that's the road to ruin. The key is to offer the *right* brand experience to each customer. Not everyone is a king, nor is everyone a peasant. It's the marketer's job to figure out who's who and to deliver what is appropriate to each.

BUILDING THE BRAND EXPERIENCE BLUEPRINT: THE PATH TO A BRAND EXPERIENCE THAT SELLS

If building the brand experience represents the best way to translate the brand architecture into reality, what steps are required? Getting marketing to step up to the challenge could easily become overwhelming. How on earth can marketing accomplish so much?

The question you should be asking yourself is this: How are we making decisions about any customer-facing investments or activities *without* an idea of what we need to do for every element of the brand experience? In other words, if you haven't adequately designed the brand experience that will deliver the benefits articulated in the brand architecture, how are customer-facing marketing investments anything but an unnecessary gamble?

This goes back to helping you answer the questions posed earlier concerning how to weigh the trade-offs between investments. Which is more important—letting your customers gain access to their purchase history or providing product configuration tools that let prospects match your core products with potential accessory items?

The answer is, of course, that you have no way of knowing unless you've adequately designed your brand experience. The name for the detailed design is a *brand experience blueprint*. While the brand architecture describes the hierarchy of benefits and attributes that drive your customer to buy, the brand experience blueprint describes in extensive detail precisely how your customer is going to *experience* all of the elements of the brand architecture—across every company touch point and every element of the marketing mix. (See Figure 4.2.)

What are the potential challenges to creating your brand experience blueprint? First things first: Creating a brand experience blueprint requires the development of a brand architecture, as

Brand Touch Points (Illustrative)	Identify Need	Evaluate Options	Buy	Use	Obtain Support
Communications					
TV	Emotional (1)	Attribute (2)	N/A	Functional (4)	N/A
Radio	Emotional (2)	Functional (2)	N/A	Functional (4)	N/A
Print	Functional (1)	Emotional (1)	Functional (4)	Emotional (1)	Functional (4)
Outdoor	Functional (2)	Functional (3)	Functional (4)	Functional (3)	N/A
Online/Email	Attribute (1)	Attribute (3)	Functional (4)	Attribute (1)	Attribute (4)
Operations					
Telemarketing	Attribute (2)	Emotional (1)	N/A	Attribute (2)	Attribute (4)
In Store	Functional (3)	Emotional (2)	Functional (4)	Functional (4)	Functional (4)
Direct Sales	Emotional (1)	Functional (1)	Functional (4)	Emotional (1)	N/A
Call Center	Functional (3)	Functional (2)	Functional (4)	Functional (4)	Functional (4)
Direct Marketing	Attribute (3)	Attribute (1)	N/A	N/A	N/A

FIGURE 4.2   Brand Experience Blueprint

explained in Chapter 2. The emotional benefits, functional benefits, and brand attributes form the core meaning of the brand that will in turn be translated into relevant context.

The steps required to create a brand experience blueprint are similar to those required to build a brand architecture, but the perspective is, of course, somewhat different. Because the brand experience blueprint designs how the *customer* should experience every stage in his/her relationship with the brand, you must go much deeper than most marketers normally do to understand the experiential elements of customer interactions. In other words, you can't just limit yourself to traditional marketing mix elements (advertising, promotion, packaging). You have to do more.

Building a brand experience blueprint requires the following steps:

1. Develop a high-level destination, aligned with the brand's destination.
2. Assess the current brand experience at a detailed level, across each element.
3. Develop hypotheses for improving the brand experience, driving to specific outcomes (including, of course, sales).
4. Validate hypotheses—focusing on achievement of key metrics.
5. Leverage validation to create a brand experience blueprint.
6. Create a blueprint release/implementation plan based on the relative difficulty/value of changes.

The first step in developing the brand experience is to *develop a destination* for each relevant element. The objective for the destination is to develop a high-level direction for the brand experience, ensuring that it's well synchronized with the benefits of the brand architecture and developing key metrics for each element along the way. The assessment phase will generate much of the detailed understanding of the way things work, but it's helpful before digging into all of the current interactions to develop some high-level direction for the brand experience. Much as with the brand architecture destination planning, destination planning for the brand experience blueprint will provide direction and alignment and will answer the questions of how a customer should think, feel, and act in each stage of the brand experience.

One other critical element of destination planning (as simple as it may sound) is to define who the customer is. While it may be an easy step in consumer goods businesses, it's not so obvious for most business purchases. If you're selling laptop computers to corporate customers, is your buyer the head of purchasing, the CIO making vendor decisions, or the user? In most instances, the definition of the customer will be expanded to include any potential customer with whom the brand might come in contact.

CASE STUDY: Nabisco

BUILDING A BRAND EXPERIENCE BLUEPRINT TO ESCAPE THE COMMODITY TRAP

To help with the demonstration of brand experience principles and practices, consider the following hypothetical case involving two companies: Nabisco and ACME Packaging. In this case, which is based on Zyman Marketing Group's experience with similar types of business-to-business relationships, ACME is a supplier to Nabisco of packaging for its numerous cookie and cracker brands (Oreo, Ritz, Wheat Thins). These two large companies work together to feed the country's desire for snacks.

Put yourself in the shoes of the ACME marketer, looking to generate more revenue from consumer packaged goods customers like Nabisco. As the head of marketing for ACME, you face a problem familiar to most business-to-business marketers. It seems that Nabisco and other consumer packaged goods (CPG) firms are forever focused on price, price, and price alone. And, if price isn't the key driver, then the company wants you to hold onto your inventory indefinitely, and then turn on a dime when production speeds up. Even worse, some of your competitors with broader product lines seem willing to cut their prices on some of your items (say, the cardboard that will be used to create the Wheat Thins box) so as to get the larger contracts for those packaging materials that are higher volume or carry a greater potential margin (say, the wrapping for Oreo packages).

The question here is, How do you build your brand experience with Nabisco to sell more, but also to bring more value to Nabisco? For many companies, even very large ones, it seems that escaping commoditization is next to impossible.

Not true. And here's the process that will help you map your escape plan.

Think back to the steps required for creating the brand experience blueprint. More specifically but still on the topic of destination planning, how do you want your customer to feel, think, and act at each stage of the brand experience? Defining the destination for a brand experience would look something like Figure 4.3 for ACME/Nabisco (from ACME's perspective).

While still at a high level, work through each step of the brand experience and develop the way you would like your customer (or targeted customer) to think, feel, and act. In addition, identify those key metrics that will serve as critical indicators of your achievement of your objectives.

For the purposes of this exercise, it is also critical to identify the key customer for each element. For large, complex purchases, many people are usually involved. While the purchasing department may be responsible for the sale, decisions may also be driven upstream

Acme Brand Touch Points		Identify Need	Evaluate Options	Buy	Use	Obtain Support
Communications	Print	Reduces breakage	Proven technology	N/A	Keeps product fresh	N/A
	Online/Email	State of the art technology	Easy to change over	Flexible terms	N/A	We come through for you
Operations	Direct Sales	Pops on the shelf	Proven - you don't want to be first	You will not lose your job	We come through for you	We come through for you
	Call Center	N/A	N/A	N/A	Fast turn around	Limited downtime

FIGURE 4.3　Brand Experience Blueprint for Nabisco/ACME

by decisions made in product marketing (such as the Ritz brand manager), production (the bakery), commercialization (the engineers that build the line for a new product), or even product development (the food technologists and professional bakers who know a lot about chemistry).

After developing a destination for the brand experience, it's time to move on to the real heavy lifting. Situation assessment requires first identifying the relevant steps of the brand experience on which to focus. For purposes of this example, let's pick an area that is often forgotten by marketers of business-to-business products or product components: the actual usage of the product by the consumer. It would be easy for ACME to focus simply on meeting the specifications provided by Nabisco, but that's not usually enough, and that's not really marketing. This is the point at which it's important to break down the element of the brand experience into its component parts.

Who Is the Customer and How Do You Connect?

For a product such as the packaging for a consumer good like a cookie or a cracker, there can be a number of different customers. First of all, the actual purchase might have taken place via Nabisco's purchasing department—probably by someone looking at current production volumes and managing inventory of packaging across a portfolio of products and bakery locations.

The customer in sales such as these is often a much broader entity than the person responsible for moving the dollars or executing the transaction.

The customer for ACME packaging is also the engineer at the bakery who happens to be responsible for ensuring that the bag-in-box machine runs properly (and doesn't result in boxes of crumbs on the grocery shelf). The package has to be able to work with the existing equipment. It has to show up on time and be easy to move onto the line at the shift change.

For the big brands in the Nabisco portfolio, of course there's a marketing or brand management individual responsible for the profit and loss for the brand. This brand manager is intensely interested in the consumer reaction to the packaging. (Does it carry colors accurately? Does it communicate the key benefits that were uncovered in the brand architecture? Does it make the cookies or crackers look delicious and inviting? Is it easy to open and close? Does it keep the product fresh? Does it prevent breakage?).

Then there's the Nabisco direct store delivery (DSD) sales force. These people are interested in how easily the package can be stacked and merchandised, because they're the ones who walk into just about every grocery store in the nation and make sure that the Fig Newtons are lined up just so. Also, they're the ones that have to create the big displays at the end of the grocery aisle, with packages of Oreos stacked to the ceiling.

Let's not forget the customer (distinct from the consumer)—in this instance, the retailer that carries Nabisco's product. Given the consolidation of retailers in the United States, each customer is enormously demanding about delivery requirements and the basic logistics of ensuring that the packages show up on time. It's a big challenge to keep Wal-Mart, Safeway, Kroger, and everyone else happy. They want answers to questions like these: Does the package communicate clearly? Does it fit in the shelf space that's been allotted? Does it keep the product fresh? Will it keep customers from bothering the store manager? Will it drive incremental revenue, or is it potentially unique or ownable for my chain of stores?

Finally, there's the consumer who actually buys Nabisco's cookies or crackers. The packaging of the product can have an enormous impact on the desire to purchase or repurchase a box of crackers or cookies. Is it resealable so that the product stays fresh? Does it look nice so a consumer can simply put it on a tray and serve guests?

You can see that when defining the brand experience blueprint, understanding who the customer is can take some time. In the context of the brand experience, they're *all* customers. Part of the complexity here is that ACME's brand benefits need to be translated into something that's relevant for every Nabisco customer.

Now you understand why taking ownership of the brand experience requires a substantial commitment from marketing.

Given that there are numerous customers who need to be considered when talking about the brand experience, let's employ the *use/educate* element as an example of how to build a brand experience blueprint. Remember that the focus here is on how to help ACME sell its packaging products to Nabisco (not on how Nabisco sells to consumers). However, it's always important to keep in mind that sometimes it's necessary to get smart about what's important to your *customer's customer* to escape the commodity trap.

With this in mind, let's consider the combination of elements in the marketing mix and the relevant customer touch points that should be used to communicate ACME's brand's benefits to Nabisco. In addition to traditional media, which are relatively rare in this sort of business-to-business environment, there are, of course, personal selling (which predominates), telemarketing, and numerous potential customer touch points to consider (web site, call center, e-mail, engineering support).

When identifying the elements of the marketing mix and the customer touch points that should be used to reach each respective customer, it's important to do more than simply indicate that a particular message needs to be delivered by a representative of ACME. If the customer is, for example, the engineer who is responsible for the bakery line that makes Wheat Thins and gets them into a plastic bag and a cardboard box, then the customer touch point might need to be an engineer deep within ACME, using a channel that hasn't been built yet.

One of the key revelations that this process uncovers is how important it is for every company to align its employees with the employees of its customers. In the retail industry, this model was widely adapted after a successful pilot between Wal-Mart and Procter & Gamble. This pilot brought together many employees of P&G who had never worked with Wal-Mart and involved logistics, product development, warehousing, sales, marketing, and so forth. This ability to align employees on this scale led to better delivery of the brand's benefits and ultimately led to more (and more profitable) sales for both parties.

Today, most companies like ACME rely solely on the interactions of their sales forces to make do. It's no wonder companies get trapped in commodity relationships. If the extent of marketing's effort is focused on reaching someone in purchasing, then everything will come down to what drives purchasing—and that is price.

What Are the Topics of Conversation?

Now that you've identified each key customer (or even desired customer) and identified the elements of the marketing mix or the specific customer touch points that should be used to reach these customers, it's time to get down to the specifics: What are the potential topics of conversation?

The real work to be done here is that for each targeted customer, you must identify the scenarios of interaction. For example, assume that the targeted customer is the bakery engineer at Nabisco. The scenarios might be something like these:

- The ACME product doesn't machine as anticipated (despite meeting specification).
- The ACME product doesn't work well with a different supplier's product (despite both meeting specification).
- The ACME product delivery does not meet expectations.
- When will more ACME product be available?
- What are my options for managing excess ACME product?
- The ACME product exceeds expectations.

These are sample potential interactions that might force a contact between a Nabisco bakery engineer and someone from ACME. These interactions form the totality of what the ACME brand means to a specific customer. The key is to identify the interactions that form the basis of the current brand experience.

Brand Experience Assessment

Once you've identified these interactions, it is time to identify where customer touch points and elements of the marketing mix play a part. You also must measure elements of the current interaction, to determine what might be driving current satisfaction or dissatisfaction.

For example, if we take one of the preceding interactions, "The ACME product does not machine as anticipated (despite meeting specification)," it is critical to develop an understanding of how often this occurs, why it usually occurs, and what the specific scenario really looks like in great detail. Does it involve certain types of packaging machines, perhaps those sold by industrial machine suppliers such as Siemens or Bosch? The more that ACME can dig into a particular scenario and understand how operations work today, the better it will be able to identify opportunities for improvement.

Even more important, by measuring elements of each scenario, ACME will be able to determine what might be holding it back from reaching the next level of sales and profits.

In addition to understanding your own scenarios, this is also the stage where it's important to look outside—perhaps outside the packaged goods industry entirely—to inject an outside perspective on what is possible. How do best-in-class companies respond when a product they've sold doesn't machine properly, despite meeting the product specification? Do they make their engineers available on an instant messenger or via some sort of hotline?

When a line goes down for longer than a minimal period, it can have a major impact on the entire supply chain and end up costing a company a lot of money. The alternative is that the engineer just makes do, recommending to purchasing that your product should be avoided in the future.

Following the situation assessment, you will have the opportunity to develop hypotheses for how to best improve each interaction. Developing compelling ideas for how to drive improved results requires a lot of creativity to identify potential *new* opportunities for bringing the brand to life. Also, the better an idea you have of the way the world works today and the aspects of life that your customer really experiences, the better informed you will be when it comes to developing the way things should be.

Having identified the key customers, the marketing mix, the customer touch points, and the interaction scenarios, you may think that all of your work is done. The situation assessment really just identifies all of the moving parts that have to be taken into consideration and then may propose direction for how to improve the weak links—usually by comparing individual parts to best practices.

This process of deconstructing the brand experience to its component parts often unleashes a lot of creative possibilities— opportunities to identify new key customers that have heretofore been ignored; opportunities to leverage new customer touch points or existing ones in a new way; and opportunities to generate, alter, or even reduce customer interactions to create better opportunities to deliver the brand's benefits within a specific context.

Once the deconstruction of the situation assessment has taken place, you're ready to begin the work of digging back into the brand's emotional benefits, functional benefits, and attributes that drive purchase intent; finding the ones that are relevant to each key customer; leveraging the best element of the marketing mix or customer touch point; and developing hypotheses for how to best address or improve each of the key customer interactions.

Continuing with the hypothetical example of the Nabisco bakery engineer who is using ACME packaging to supply the carton that carries

Wheat Thins, the output of ACME's situation assessment for this specific scenario might be something like the following.

Current Brand Interactions—Key Customer—Nabisco Bakery Engineer

- ACME product doesn't machine as anticipated (despite meeting spec)
  - Customer touch points:
    - Web site (product specs)
    - Call center (calls from bakery engineer routed to sales rep)
    - Shipping documents provide copy of product specification
  - Marketing mix:
    - Print ads in baking trade magazine
  - Relevant benefits:
    - Emotional
      - None communicated
    - Functional
      - Generic ACME corporate message—ACME offers state-of-the-art capabilities in packaging
    - Attributes
      - Product delivered as "meeting spec"
    - Desired outcomes/metrics
      - Limited production downtime for Nabisco
      - High degree of satisfaction by bakery engineer
      - Communication of satisfaction from bakery engineer to brand manager
      - Communication of satisfaction from bakery engineer to purchasing

Brand Experience Hypotheses

Once you've completed the situation assessment of your brand experience, which essentially involves taking inventory of every interaction, with every key customer, across every touch point and element of the marketing mix, you're then able to apply everything that you've learned along the way to generate hypotheses about how to improve the overall experience. This improvement will come in achievement of specific outcomes for each element of the brand experience and ultimately in sales.

It's important that the primary objectives of sales and profitability never become too distant in your calculations. While it can be tempting to measure success with metrics such as the satisfaction of the bakery engineer in the ACME/Nabisco example, that satisfaction is only relevant if it's a driver of additional sales. In other words, any element of the brand experience is important only to the extent that a causal relationship with sales can be identified. If it's not a driver of sales (or profitability), then it doesn't really belong in the marketer's radar.

The hypotheses you develop depend on the knowledge you uncover from your brand experience assessment. To follow through on the ACME/Nabisco example, you would generate hypotheses such as the following (remember, you're in the shoes of ACME, marketing to cookie and cracker giant Nabisco):

- Providing an engineering support service to Nabisco bakery engineers would improve service and overall satisfaction.
  - Develop concept details, channels, staffing, and pricing for test.
- Working more closely with product designers *before* the spec is developed would eliminate machining problems with ACME products, including working with packaging equipment makers.
  - Identify marketing mix elements and customer touch points to provide this input up front, before spec is created.
- Improving the web site and providing instant messaging support (and connection to in-house ACME engineers) would provide the fastest response to potential problems.
- Providing "working with ACME packaging" training would reduce overall call volume and eliminate potential downtime from machining problems.

These are, of course, hypothetical examples, but they give you an idea of the types of hypotheses that you must develop. These hypotheses then must be validated to determine not only whether they have an impact on a particular metric—say, production engineer satisfaction—

but, most important, whether it's possible to make a connection between the measured outcome for an element of the brand experience and sales.

Hypotheses Validation

Validation of the hypotheses that will drive improvement of the brand experience and result in the brand experience blueprint—the specification, as it were, for what you would like your customer's brand experience to be—depends on the specifics of your business and the specifics of your particular hypotheses.

In some instances, you will need to resort to the type of quantitative research described in Chapter 2, similar to the research required to develop a brand architecture. However, in many cases, you may be able to leverage your living experiment, meaning your current business operations, to run a pilot or regional test.

One of the beauties of focusing on the brand experience is that the subject isn't something esoteric or distant from your company. The topic is literally every interaction with every potential customer, so it is something that will likely be near and dear already to someone in your company. Rest assured, if the Nabisco bakery engineer is unhappy, then your sales team focused on Nabisco is likely to know all about it, or at least have an idea that it's a problem.

This validation is very much a part of delivering on the new science of marketing. It gives you an opportunity to conduct an experiment and then incorporate the results into your brand experience blueprint.

Develop the Brand Experience Blueprint

Once you've validated your hypotheses, you finally have everything you need to draw up your brand experience blueprint.

Across every element of the brand experience for every key customer, for every scenario, and for every customer touch point and marketing mix element, what do you want the *experience* to be, from your customer's perspective? In building this map of the total relationship or brand experience, just as in building a home or a skyscraper, the outcome of a brand architecture and a brand experience blueprint is the total picture, both from an inside-out perspective (what are the benefits that really communicate the essence of *my* brand?) and an outside-in perspective (what does the customer actually experience when he/she interacts with my brand?).

The brand experience blueprint will become the marketer's laboratory, laying out every potential interaction with every potential customer or customer segment. The old days of buying media and hoping that advertising is getting something done are over. The new science requires that marketers take ownership of the brand experience. The only way to really do that is to understand what that brand experience is and to stake out a direction for creating the ideal brand experience by creating a brand experience blueprint. With this blueprint in hand, marketing has the tool that it needs to push, prod, and cajole every other part of the company, so that whenever anyone interacts with a customer, there's a specific desired outcome to correspond with the interaction. That interaction is no longer something marketing has to leave to the whims of other departments.

These days, every customer interaction is an opportunity to sell. Isn't it time that you took control of your brand experience? Why would anyone want to leave something so important to chance?

MARKETER'S SCIENTIFIC METHOD: RESHAPING THE COMPANY IN MARKETING'S IMAGE

The way to improve your company's brand experience is to develop the requirements for what that experience should be—across every element, from the very first consideration all the way through support. Your customer's experience with your brand is far too important to be left to chance.

To create your company's Brand Experience Blueprint, you should follow these steps.

Step 1: Develop a High-Level Destination, Aligned with the Brand's Destination

Don't assume that just because you're about to invest a huge amount of money everyone on your team is in sync with the strategy. Such assumptions inevitably turn out to be wrong. Make the time to ensure that this alignment takes place, or it usually doesn't happen.

Step 2: Assess the Current Brand Experience at a Detailed Level, Across Each Element

Assessing the brand experience requires a significant commitment of time and resources. The more you understand your customer's current experience with your brand, the smarter you will be at crafting that experience as you move forward. Look to evaluate the brand experience not just with qualititative measures but with hard numbers: How long does it take to get X done? How many customers are experiencing Y? How many people does the company employ just to address interaction Z? Be sure to apply measures of cost, time, and quality to the current brand experience. This evaluation must be done with the potential investment in mind that will set things as you want them to be.

Step 3: Develop Hypotheses for Improving the Brand Experience, Driving to Specific Outcomes (Including Sales)

Put on your thinking caps and grab every creative person you know. This is your chance to reinvent the way your customer experiences your brand. Don't be constrained by the way things are, and be open to alternative models from any industry.

Step 4: Validate Hypotheses, Focusing on Achievement of Key Metrics

Don't forget: Your business is your laboratory. You have an opportunity to learn right on the spot, maybe by carving out a location or region, or maybe by using one of your hot dog stands to validate some of your hypotheses about the changes in the brand experience that will drive your sales higher.

Step 5: Leverage Validation to Create the Brand Experience Blueprint

Creating the brand experience blueprint is much like the work an architect does. It requires a lot of attention to detail. The blueprint itself may change, but it becomes the bible for how things are supposed to be. You may move a beam here or maybe decide to rewire there, but your brand experience blueprint should form the core of your customer's experience with your brand.

Step 6: Create a Blueprint Release/Implementation Plan Based on Relative Difficulty/Value of Changes

Once you have the plan, you can't just slide it in a drawer and hope that something happens. This step requires that you think through the sort of changes in your business model that will be required to make this plan a reality. Do you have the right people, processes, and technology to bring your brand experience blueprint to life? Remember, if you're not going to build it up to code, then you're just wasting your time.

5

PLUG MARKETING INTO CRM

So now we have defined the brand experience as the container for every customer interaction with your brand—across all physical touch points (e.g., stores, call centers, direct sales) as well as across all elements of the traditional marketing mix (e.g., advertising, promotions, packaging). If your brand represents the specific emotional and functional benefits that you communicate and deliver in providing a product or service to your targeted customers, then your brand experience is the gauge of the actual experience your customers have across every potential interaction with your company and its people—from the moment they contemplate a specific need through their usage of the product and their potential need for support.

At this point, you might jump to the conclusion that a robust enterprise information system that helps you manage customer relationships at every touch point is the perfect solution for developing productive, profitable brand experiences. Perhaps you are tempted to go out and buy the fanciest, most expensive system you can find. Please don't fall into that trap. Tell the software vendor that you'll call back next week and read on.

JUST MANAGING CUSTOMER RELATIONSHIPS ISN'T NEARLY ENOUGH

Customer relationships taken out of the context of your company's brand are irrelevant. Enterprise-wide information systems like customer relationship management (CRM) can be powerful and drive a strategic advantage only if they provide a better way to deliver on the promise of your brand. Delivering on this promise requires that before you invest one dollar in software or process changes, you develop your brand's architecture and convert that into a blueprint for the experience you want customers to have with your brand. A brand experience blueprint describes how a brand's benefits are to be delivered and represents the *real business requirements* for any CRM-related project.

> *How can any CRM implementation deliver on a brand's promise if the primary brand benefits don't form the starting point for designing potential CRM functionality?*

It's time to face some hard facts about customer relationship management, and the way that it is being pursued by many companies today. Plain and simple, CRM just isn't getting the job done. It's the subject of all the talk on web sites, at conferences, in nervous boardrooms: CRM isn't driving top-line results. And everyone's getting worried—from the companies that have sunk millions into buying the software, to the software providers themselves, to the IT services companies that see CRM as their best chance for post-dot-bomb survival.

One problem is that CRM can offer some deceptive short-term success. Implement the sales force automation (SFA) elements of CRM, and you're likely to see a bump in sales thanks to newfound process efficiencies. But, like changing tires at the Indy 500, it's not enough to win you the race—it's just enough to keep you from getting lapped by your competition. You might have happier customers, but are they buying more from you? Your salespeople might be engaged in more selling activities and doing a better job of reporting their progress, but are they actually selling more for you? Outside of SFA, most companies struggle to determine how to monitor and track interactions and messaging across all customer touch points—and, from there, to actually *make* some money. Let's take a closer look at how to do just that.

THE PERILS AND PROMISE OF CRM

CRM isn't always a low-return investment. Quite the contrary; it serves a useful purpose when employed correctly. And it's easy enough to see what motivates a company to make an investment in CRM. When companies see customer acquisition costs rising and conversion rates decreasing, when potential marketing channels proliferate and companies need more productivity, CRM is a useful investment that has the potential to drive significant returns. From a technology perspective, CRM delivers key functional benefits such as centralization of customer data, access to that data across the enterprise in a secure and private way, and execution support across multiple channels.

However, amazingly, an estimated 70 percent of CRM projects don't produce measurable business benefits, according to a study performed by Berkeley Enterprise Partners. Even worse, 64 percent of CRM users in one sample lacked the techniques to even measure the business value of their CRM systems, and less than *10 percent* of companies can measure tangible ROI in CRM. CRM efforts also suffer from scope or budget creep; almost a third of companies running CRM have had to revise their budget upward, by an average of 46 percent (source: Meta Group).

The current situation is even more disturbing when you consider the testimony of customers of industry-leading CRM solution providers such as Siebel Systems. Findings recently published by Nucleus Research ("Assessing the Real ROI from Siebel," September 2002) revealed that 61 percent of Siebel customers interviewed did not believe they achieved a positive ROI from their Siebel deployment. It is important to note that this research did not profile a statistically significant sample of Siebel customers—and was never designed to. The reason for this is simple: This research was designed to focus on *Siebel's reference customers only*. To put this in the proper context, the customers surveyed were the individuals highlighted on Siebel's web site and profiled as achieving success with their CRM deployment. In other words, even Siebel's *best customers* are not realizing the benefits promised by CRM.

Table 5.1   Most CRM Projects Don't Meet Expectations

Expectation	Results to Date
One view of the customer	Multiple, functional views of customer
Improved overall customer satisfaction	Only improved experience locally
Increased customer satisfaction	Improved efficiencies
Reduced customer defection and increased customer loyalty	Increase in retention accompanied by increase in downward migration
Profitable growth	Reduced customer conversion and market contraction

The sad fact is that despite great intentions and breakthrough technologies, most CRM initiatives do not meet business (or customer) expectations (see Table 5.1).

CRM AND THE MARKETING GAP

The problem is a matter of focus. To this point, CRM applications have focused largely on the orchestration and analysis of customer interaction processes (that is, sales and service automation) and direct marketing (a.k.a. campaign management). In the grand scheme of things, CRM has just scratched the surface and is still a long way from transforming the way companies create value for customers. For instance, CRM hasn't yet been fully employed to support such essential marketing activities as strategic planning, market sensing, customer message management, brand architecture development, brand management, product development, and marketing investment management. Furthermore, CRM has also tended to make companies overly e-focused—centering their attention too heavily on the Internet, even though traditional selling channels, such as face to face, business partners, and telechannels, still account for more than 95 percent of revenues (source: Meta Group). But before diving further into the possibilities for closing the gap between CRM and marketing, let's consider some historical perspective.

Before the age of CRM, marketing departments invested all of their time and money trying to land current and potential customers when they *weren't* interacting with the company—they were watching television, reading magazines, strolling through airports, and so forth. Once a company located its target customers, it would zero in with messaging that would supposedly sink in far enough to help customers make the right purchasing decisions when the time came.

But now that CRM has arrived, marketing has a powerful weapon it doesn't even think to use. CRM systems give marketers the tools to catch and communicate to customers at any and all times during which they interact with your company, whether you're running a lemonade stand or a multinational corporation with web sites, retail stores, distributors, and call centers. A marketer's most cherished dream is having the opportunity to fish where the fish are. But it seems that no one has told the marketers where the pond is located.

Even worse, some companies continue to invest in CRM efforts even though they've been unable to make a clear connection between their company's brand promise and the use of CRM. This is like driving faster when you're lost, and it can lead you to all sorts of strange places.

You may not believe it, but some companies are so focused on building great relationships with their customers that they've forgotten that CRM is all about selling. They prefer to believe that if only they could create a great relationship with their customers, then the dollars would magically flow in.

Nonsense. Create customer relationships all you want—if they're not leading to sales, they're not worth the effort. This airy foolishness about the value of relationships is why CRM investments don't pay off. It's already difficult enough to sell more every month, every quarter, every year . . . and it's that much harder if you're merely tossing your brand name to the winds and hoping it will connect with some customer somewhere.

However, if you've developed a productive, profitable *brand experience* for your customers (see Chapter 4), you've created a marketing asset that can be used over and over again. In other words, if marketing can teach your customers to associate compelling emotional and functional benefits with your brand, then you've got something to build on. And if you use the architecture of your brand and the desired brand experience blueprint to inform the design and implementation of your CRM capability, you're in business.

Sounds logical, seems pretty straightforward, but somewhere along the way companies are getting off track. Why? A primary reason is that CRM has been focused (and financially justified) predominantly on creating operational efficiencies for the enterprise rather than doing things differently from competitors in a way that delivers unique value to customers.

CRM CREATES OPERATIONAL EFFICIENCIES FOR EVERYBODY

Developing a business case for CRM that promises significant improvements in operational efficiency is not a bad place to start (see Figure 5.1). Companies must achieve, maintain, and extend *best practices* in sales, service, and marketing activities in order to be competitive. Furthermore, to justify the multi-million-dollar budget required to invest in the most up-to-date hardware, CRM software,

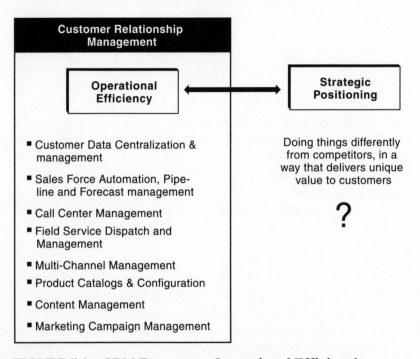

FIGURE 5.1   CRM Focuses on Operational Efficiencies

and networking technologies, you're going to have to drive out some cost savings and productivity gains. Even more important, you must show how you will eliminate waste, defects, and delays in *serving customers*. Increases in customer satisfaction and productivity gains form the basis for just about everyone's CRM business case. But here's the punchline: Improving operational efficiency using CRM is necessary to achieving superior profitability, but it is not sufficient on its own to create a sustainable competitive advantage. You will soon discover that CRM generates absolute but not relative improvement within your industry—and competitive convergence will happen sooner than you think! In other words, you'll improve your business performance, but in a way that your competitors can emulate and imitate very easily. After all, *CRM technologies are available to everyone.*

So why are most CRM initiatives failing to generate sufficient returns on investment? Interestingly enough, looking at the component letters of the acronym itself can reveal some of the flaws in the thinking about customer relationship management. Most companies have focused on the "M," forgotten about the "C," and failed to recognize that marketing drives the "R." And there's a letter missing altogether: the "B" for brand. If the collection of emotional and functional benefits and product attributes that drive purchase intent aren't the primary driver of your CRM strategy, then CRM is de facto disconnected from the company's core asset—its brand. Simply put, CRM initiatives have focused on *managing* customer relationships, not *developing* them by delivering specific brand benefits. The CRM initiatives that are generating the greatest business results are the ones whereby companies are using technology to enable the development of productive, profitable brand-based relationships with their customers—not just *managing* the customer interaction in a manner that is more efficient for the company. Companies that use CRM to generate a deep understanding and insightful anticipation of their customers' needs and wants can realize even more substantial returns on their CRM investments.

However, if you're not careful and you implement CRM simply to manage your customers rather than delivering on your brand promise, you can end up doing much more harm than good.

Here's a simple example: It's Christmastime, and a large toy retailer has offered fantastic promotions if you use its web site to make your purchases. The company has set up a fantastic new e-channel, which allows you, the valued customer, to stay out of the busy stores at Christmastime and make all of your purchases from the comfort of your living room. Sounds like a great customer relationship experience. However, when you try to reach the site, you discover that it's so popular that it can't serve you and you're asked to come back later. What does this interaction communicate about the retailer's brand? Was this new e-channel designed and developed to deliver on the brand promise across every customer interaction? When the actual customer interaction—a web site outage in this case—conflicts severely with a brand's key emotional benefit (i.e., makes you a better parent by ensuring you can get your child what he or she wants), tempers are going to flare. What was intended as a way to extend a brand's benefits through a new channel can quickly become a way to deteriorate the value of the brand altogether.

Here's another example: After a lengthy and painful negotiation with a car salesman, you're sitting in the finance manager's office at the car dealership, trying to secure financing so that you can drive the car of your dreams off the lot today. In the middle of the arduous process of collecting information about you to process your loan application, he shoves a credit card application in front of you and suggests that you fill it out. What brand promise is being delivered on by the auto finance company? In their rush to achieve the utopian state of *cross-selling*, financial services companies have forgotten that consumers often have no interest in *cross-buying*.

Both of these are examples of CRM run amok, CRM functionality in search of a marketing strategy. Many companies are using CRM to streamline interactions for *their benefit* and to bundle disparate product pitches in an effort to penetrate deeper into their customers' wallets. By simply asking customers what they need or want, companies can discover that, as in the example, negotiating for and buying a new car is stressful enough and is not the best time to confuse matters by asking buyers to make another decision! That said, the same customer may be willing to listen to that credit card offer after the deal is concluded—and if it is put in the context of a real consumer need, concern, or benefit ("You know, there might come a day when you can't make a car payment. . . . Wouldn't it be nice to know that you have the ability to pay on credit and not risk losing your dream car?"). Unfortunately, CRM for many companies has become synonymous with cross-selling you more of their stuff (more about this in Chapter 6).

CRM CAN CREATE SUSTAINABLE
COMPETITIVE ADVANTAGE

The lessons are becoming more obvious: Just because everyone can use CRM doesn't mean everyone *should use it in the same way.* Companies can achieve a sustainable advantage through the use of CRM, but they need to understand what it's going to cost them in terms of financial investment, strategic trade-offs, and relinquished opportunity. Traditional business thinking focuses on the ability to imitate competitors, since standard barriers to imitation are often low. True sustainability arises when competitors do not *want* to imitate because of the trade-offs they would need to make to keep pace with an industry segment leader. As Dr. Michael Porter of the Harvard Business School notes, "True competitive advantage can be sustained only when operating at a lower cost, commanding a premium price, or both." When approached properly, a CRM initiative can help you do just that.

Consider the examples of Southwest Airlines, Enterprise Rent-A-Car, and IKEA. Each one of these companies generates a relatively higher level of performance (in terms of profitability) in its respective industry because each has secured an advantage that others cannot afford (or do not want) to imitate. Southwest Airlines has made specific trade-offs in serving its customers. Yes, it offers low fares. But Southwest also doesn't have the burden of running hub operations, it flies only one type of aircraft (Boeing 737s), and it doesn't offer meals, frills, or paper tickets, so it can guarantee 15-minute gate turns. Similar focused strategies have been carved out by Enterprise (located away from airports, serving longer-term rental customers) and IKEA (pick out your furniture in a warehouse environment, haul it to the counter, pay for it, and put it together yourself). Can United Airlines, Hertz, and Bombay Company easily imitate and develop these types of relationships with customers? Would they want to?

These companies use various forms of CRM technologies in creating value for their customers. But clearly, CRM shows the greatest results when it delivers new and unique value to customers, and when the brand promise and the operational delivery are completely aligned. Does it make sense for Southwest Airlines to invest heavily in data systems that track the meal preferences of its customers? Of course not, but it makes sense for United. Does it make sense for Southwest to invest in automated systems for expediting gate turns, cleaning its 737s and refueling to ensure on-time departure? Absolutely. Does it make sense for United? One could argue that since many of its planes do not depart on time, its customers have come to expect a certain amount of delay. In fact, it might make sense to invest more in CRM technologies that keep the customers informed of delays before they get to the airport and keep them occupied in the gatehouse when delays inevitably occur. Unless you do the research to deeply understand the needs and wants of customers, or, most important, that combination of emotional and functional benefits that actually drive purchase intent, you can easily end up investing in the wrong CRM functionality—just because everyone else has made the same mistake.

FROM CUSTOMER DATA TO ACTIONABLE CUSTOMER INSIGHTS

One of the pleasant outcomes of implementing CRM across your enterprise is that you end up with a tremendous amount of data about your customers. You will likely have more interesting facts and figures about your customers and their buying habits than you ever imagined possible. Then, when you integrate CRM with the data available through ERP applications, there is no end to the depth, availability, and various aggregations of customer data now available to companies. Of course, you still face the daunting challenge of making sense of it all. And even more important, you must be able to act on that information to drive sales and profitability in order to justify the investment you have made in the technology. This is often more easily said than done.

Why? Because there is a big difference between the raw *customer usage data* that most CRM and ERP systems provide and the *actionable customer insights* that you need to drive your business (see Figure 5.2). For instance, most commercially available CRM solutions are very good at tracking descriptive and quantitative data about reach and response rates on marketing campaigns, what and when salespeople sell, what and when customers buy, and what and when customers are being served. The major questions still remaining for most enterprises are these:

~ Why are salespeople selling (or not selling)?
~ Why are customers buying (or not buying)?

~ What do I have to do or say to attract more customers?
~ What do I have to do or say to get customers to buy more of my product?
~ What do I have to do or say to get customers to pay more for my product than for that of the competition?
~ What are customers and noncustomers saying about their experience with our company and our brands?

In other words, how do you translate all of these interesting facts about your customers and noncustomers into *something that you can do today to increase profitability?*

Consider this example: The director of marketing for a branded laser printer manufacturer receives a monthly download of data from the company's in-house CRM system on the volume of toner cartridges that is sold each month across the various retail channels of distribution. In recent months, she has noticed a steep decline in the purchase of toner cartridges with one of the regional office supply wholesalers. The decline varies by geographic location, but, generally speaking, volume is down across the board in this channel. The director of marketing investigates further and discovers that this particular wholesaler has been experimenting with a new service to recycle and refill cartridges on behalf of its national retail accounts. This action is clearly cannibalizing share for the manufacturer, but even more frustrating is the fact that the manufacturer runs a recycling service of its own for its large national distributors.

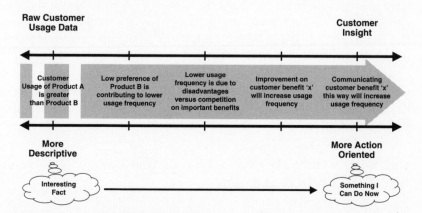

FIGURE 5.2   From Customer Usage Data to Actionable Customer Insights

The wholesaler is now in direct competition with the manufacturer! As you might imagine, the dialogue between the manufacturer and the wholesaler quickly grows heated from this point forward. The manufacturer claims that the wholesaler is violating the terms of their distribution contract, and the wholesaler argues that the cartridge itself is a commodity and that recycling is a higher-margin business for it. But here is a more important question: Who is missing from this example? The end user, of course. Clearly, the idea of a recycled, more environmentally friendly, perhaps less expensive toner cartridge is appealing to the end user. The wholesaler and its retail partners have revealed this insight through experimentation. Even though the manufacturer was a major player in this business, it was so distant from the end user that it was unable to uncover and act upon the insight and was blindly motivated to continue selling more new cartridges even though it had been in the recycling business for some of its larger direct accounts.

This is the classic trap for manufacturers that attempt to implement CRM in a multitiered distribution system: They are often so distant from their end users that the raw customer usage data is highly retrospective and lacks sufficient perspective on attitudes and behavior to provide usable insights. Even if you are lucky enough to reveal a customer insight, if the data is not timely, it may be too late to take advantage of the opportunity.

An effective CRM implementation in this type of environment would span the entirety of the end users' brand experience with the laser printer, taking into account the various replenishable products and services that they may require. In this type of implementation, the manufacturer could end up adding a tremendous amount of value to its channel partners beyond just supplying high-quality products and services. For example, the manufacturer could use CRM analytics to reveal that communicating various types of benefits and capabilities of the laser printer will encourage increased usage—and, in turn, the need to replenish the cartridges.

USE CRM TO PLUG IN TO THE DIALOGUE WITH INFLUENTIALS

The Internet, mobile solutions, and other associated new media have complicated matters for many enterprises by accelerating the need for timeliness of insights into customer needs and wants. Customer and consumer trends now have the potential to turn on a dime thanks to the power of the Internet to seamlessly spread information by electronic word of mouth. Moreover, wireless communication devices and mobile business applications on these devices allow consumers to spread the word anytime and anywhere. At sites such as www.bizrate.com and www.epinions.com, customers post their kudos and complaints, describe the ups and downs of their relationships, and profile their experiences with various brands and companies in every category imaginable. These people are not afraid to voice their opinions, chronicle their experiences in excruciating detail, alert other consumers to the hazards of working with the company, and give pointers on how the company could have better met their needs. As a result, concepts such as brand preference, reach, and loyalty are much more complicated now. They are far more amorphous, with the potential to change whenever and wherever a customer interacts with your brand—offline, via wireline, and wirelessly. Of greatest concern is the fact that you may not be in control of the dialogue about your brands. Your CRM initiative may be lulling you into a false sense of security, so that you believe you are getting the whole story at traditional sales and service touch points.

In its ongoing research of this subject, Burson-Marsteller has been tracking a particularly powerful subgroup of consumers that it calls *E-fluentials*. These consumers, representing about 10 percent of the U.S. population, were among the first to explore and understand the inherent power of the Internet as a channel for commerce and communication. According to the research, E-fluentials have "a disproportionate impact, relative to their size, on the buzz surrounding brands, products and services." The research report goes on to point out that E-fluentials "have a say in the purchasing decisions—online and offline—of approximately 155 million consumers."

Given the influential power of such a group of consumers and their potential to provide insights into the emerging needs and wants of millions of customers, it seems only logical that a company should identify this segment within its own customer base and target these customers with very specific marketing and CRM initiatives to break into the dialogue.

A WORD TO THE WISE

As demonstrated by the cross-selling examples earlier in this chapter, you may be tempted to leverage some of your newfound knowledge about your customers, tap into the dialogue of your influentials, and end up abusing your customer relationships. Be careful: You're walking a fine line here. It's one thing to be genuinely interested in anticipating the needs and wants of your customers, but it becomes something completely different if you use that knowledge to inundate them with offers that are designed primarily to help you to meet your objectives.

If properly implemented and focused, CRM can create sustainable competitive advantages for your business. However, in order to do so, marketers must close the gap that exists between the marketing function and today's approach to CRM implementations:

~ CRM applications must be tailored and configured to deliver on the benefits articulated in the brand architecture and to implement the brand experience blueprint for each brand across all channels, reinforcing the drivers of differentiation and preference.
~ CRM analytics must be enhanced to go beyond just gathering and reporting customer data. You must tailor this data to generate proper context and understanding which in turn will help you improve the brand experience for your customers.
~ You must connect CRM capability with marketing's ability to understand the dynamic nature of consumer trends. By combining these strengths, you can take control of the dialogue with influentials and trendsetters to understand and predict the consumer behaviors that ultimately drive purchase intent.

GETTING THE PAYBACK ON CRM INVESTMENTS

The key message here is that CRM will pay you back if it builds on and reinforces an existing strength, advantage, or core competence. Furthermore, you can expect high returns from initiatives that use CRM to reinforce trade-offs and solidify brand positioning, exploit your skills in customer analytics, provide unique access to customer or market data, enable strong service cultures, or accelerate merger and acquisition strategies.

But don't get hung up on measuring every twist and turn of your CRM initiative. Believe it or not, CRM projects underpinned by rigorous ROI analysis are more likely to fail than those in which the numbers are less rigid! The reason is that in the rush to assemble rigorous business cases to justify CRM implementations, significant attention is paid to the things that are easy to measure (typically, cost savings) and less attention is paid to the revenue-generating and customer-driven parts of the equation. In extreme cases, marketing and the customer demand creation side of the equation are completely ignored. There's an old saying that describes this situation: You get what you measure. A rigorous business case focused on cost savings will yield exactly that: cost savings. Furthermore, if marketing and the voice of the customer are excluded from the process, there will be a tendency for the focus of the CRM initiative to shift inward. Certainly, a business case that is looser in terms of assumptions around increases in revenue and ultimate cost to serve customers may not meet with accolades from the CFO, but it will clearly indicate that the focus of the CRM vision has shifted beyond the four walls of the company. Simply put, a leading indicator for success is a *less rigid business case* in which marketing perspectives have been fully integrated across every aspect of CRM design and implementation.

THE OTHER OPTION

Of course, there's always the option to do nothing, to sit tight and stay on your current course with CRM. In this scenario, where no company in an industry does anything to distinguish its offerings to customers, price becomes the only definition of customer value, as opposed to specialization, convenience, service, or other forms of differentiation. As a result, companies seek to dominate the entire market instead of establishing uniqueness and making trade-offs to capture a well-chosen submarket. It may be a good idea if you're the leader in your industry and you're looking to drive off your weaker competitors. But if not, it's a tough competitive model to reverse, and your entire industry will suffer the consequences. Of course, in any scenario, you must make sure that you're not *overinvesting* in

CRM—developing neat new functionality for which you get no acknowledgment or reward from customers.

SMART COMPANIES WILL SWIM IN A DIFFERENT DIRECTION

The whole world is enjoying the CRM feeding frenzy. Trouble is, most companies are going at CRM like one fish in a school: watching tentatively to see what their equally fishy competitors are doing and then going about CRM work exactly the same way. Or, even worse, they're implementing one vendor's version of *industry best practices* in hopes of minimizing the short-term aggravation, implementation risks, and expense.

The hard truth is that acting just like the other members of your industry is no way to develop a winning brand strategy, to increase sales, and to earn sustained, superior returns for your shareowners. While there is no one right way to use CRM effectively, the one wrong way to use CRM is to use it just like your competition. Each company's take on CRM must be driven by its brand architecture, the differentiated promise its brand makes to its targeted customers. If a company's use of CRM is simply to change technology and processes, then the company has done nothing to build a defensible asset that drives benefits for customers while keeping competitors at bay.

One day soon, every fish in the school is going to look around and realize that since everyone now has CRM, nobody has a technological advantage. And if you're not putting your brand to work to differentiate yourself and sell across all touch points, you're never going to outswim or evolve into a shark.

CASE STUDY: Toshiba

INTEGRATING MARKETING SCIENCE INTO CRM

Toshiba is a perfect example of how to integrate marketing techniques with customer relationship management in order to make a powerful appeal to the customer. Toshiba is a key player in the hypercompetitive U.S. PC industry, where six leading vendors control nearly 60 percent of the market. Toshiba's executives understood the industry's growing move toward differentiation strategies and direct-selling channels and resolved to compete head-on to make Toshiba a major player in the changing PC arena.

Customer loyalty, once a hallmark of the computer industry, is now at an all-time low. Customers will no longer select a computer simply based on the name on the box. The physical differences between personal computers are minor, while the differences in relevant service offerings—including distribution and customer support—are often vast. Indeed, most major PC competitors are considering their nonhardware divisions as sources of competitive advantage—or disadvantage.

Toshiba picked up on the fact that change is necessary from market and consumer research, and decided to reorient itself as a world-class total computer solutions provider. The company, recognizing the shopping power its customers now wield thanks to the Internet, decided to focus on customers at every level of its organization. Toshiba thus used CRM to help establish a company-wide *pull* strategy, encouraging and allowing customers to source what they need from Toshiba rather than *pushing* products onto them.

With the vast resources available through CRM technologies, Toshiba developed a variety of total customer solutions packages, each tailored to the specific needs of its customers. Toshiba established an enterprise-wide strategic positioning strategy, coupled with the CRM solutions, that allows and encourages its customers to source the products they want, configured in the way they want, and when they need them.

Prior to implementing the CRM systems, Toshiba conducted a complete analysis of its internal operations. It uncovered disturbing inefficiencies, such as the fact that its sales reps were spending up to 40 percent of their time conducting administrative activities. Furthermore, customer information was maintained on as many as 18 different external and internal data management systems.

In order to maximize its efficiency, Toshiba rolled out a series of large-scale strategic initiatives designed to effect dramatic changes. The rollout included a supply chain management initiative, an Internet initiative, and a CRM strategy, all of which were organized around the demands and needs of the customer.

Toshiba implemented the CRM system in order to establish consistency and unity across all internal and external touch points. With the CRM foundation in place, Toshiba developed predictive models of customer behavior and demand, which in turn generated significant changes in Toshiba's structure, management, and operations.

The CRM initiative set Toshiba firmly on the path to profitability. With a new focus on customer demand, Toshiba can now drive and meet that demand through its centralized customer contact system. The company has an improved ability to sell products and services to current and prospective target customers. It also has a tighter rein on its finances through a better management of revenue targets, increased process efficiencies, and a reduction of costs.

Technology companies have little control over the broad economic upswings and downturns in their industries. But they can control the way in which they prepare for and respond to the demands of businesses and consumers. With a fully implemented CRM system and a comprehensive marketing plan, Toshiba has a firm handle on its market—and its future.

MARKETER'S SCIENTIFIC METHOD: PLUGGING MARKETING INTO CRM

If you're currently running or considering the implementation of a CRM solution, you need to start by asking yourself two hard questions:

1. How do you use all of your customer touch points to *sell more?*
2. How does your CRM solution track each customer message used, as well as its effectiveness by customer touch point, so that you can *improve* your answer to question 1?

You'll note that we used the "s" word—*sell*—in question 1. That might lead you to believe that this issue belongs in the sales arena. Wrong. We're talking marketing, pure and simple.

Marketing is all about closing the sale before the deal even takes place. It's about selling more stuff, to more people, more often, for more money, more efficiently. And it's not a province where IT can give you the best answers for your money.

So it's up to you in marketing to do some homework and figure out how to maximize your CRM return.

Step 1: Develop a Penetrating Understanding of Your Brand Positioning

We described how to be the architect of your brand in Chapter 2. The brand architecture embodies all of the benefits that drive customer purchase intent. Put more simply: Know what your brand means and how to communicate that meaning to your customers. If you aren't doing this, you're just throwing away money.

Step 2: Leverage This Understanding to Develop the Ideal Brand Experience for Customers

Flesh out the brand experience your customer has by creating the specific content, functionality, or messages that are delivered through the marketing mix and at each customer touch point. This brand experience blueprint, discussed in Chapter 4, addresses all aspects of the way your company interacts with your customer, including downstream, postpurchase interactions about how to use or service what you sell.

Step 3: Inform CRM Design and Implementation Decision Making

Now you are prepared to evaluate and make informed decisions regarding various CRM technologies and implementation alternatives. Making the right choices regarding what you will (and won't) implement with CRM is at the heart of building productive, profitable relationships with your customers.

Marketers need to take advantage of opportunities outside the traditional domain of marketing to build brand preference. The concept of brand experience bridges the gap between marketing's traditional domain of the marketing mix and the emerging focus on customer relationship management.

It is not about radical repositioning of your marketing efforts—it is about taking a new look at what you've already got.

6

CROSS-MARKET TO CROSS-SELL

One of the most basic tenets of marketing is that it's always easier to sell to the customers you already have than to those you don't. Encouraging the customer already in the store to pick up an extra item or two on the way to the register is much easier than pulling someone in off the street. It's also much more profitable over time; it costs 5 to 12 times more to acquire a new customer than to retain an existing one. Once you've won over a customer the first time, it's always easier to sell them additional products and services because you've already gotten over one of the most difficult hurdles: *The customer knows you and knows what your brand stands for.*

However, persuading a customer to buy disparate products and services from you can be a daunting challenge. For example, many financial services companies struggle to convince their customers to consolidate all of their assets with one institution (e.g., savings, investments, insurance, home mortgage, auto loans, and so forth). In most cases, customers just don't understand the offers and fear putting all of their eggs in one basket. Furthermore, most financial institutions have focused on *bundling products* that they want to sell, rather than *bundling benefits* that would be of value to their customers.

Obviously, over the long run, you're going to benefit from holding on to your existing customers. Loyal customers tend to make more purchases, are more likely to accept price premiums than newcomers, and are less costly and time consuming to service. You've already rewarded your customers with quality service and products; now it's their turn to reward you with loyalty, flexibility, and openness to new ideas—if you're bold enough to ask them.

Sell more to those you know. It's such a simple idea, and yet so many companies completely miss out on this vastly untapped resource. Or they abuse it by failing to truly understand the needs and wants of their customers, bombarding them with annoying offers in order to meet internal cross-sell objectives. The fact is, most companies have been looking at the problem from the wrong perspective. It's not about cross-selling, it's about activating customer intent to *cross-buy*. And to do that, you first need to understand how to cross-market— making your existing customers even *better* customers. You've already got them in the door; now make sure they take a couple more things with them before they go.

HISTORICAL PERSPECTIVE ON CROSS-SELLING

Savvy companies have been cross-selling for as long as commerce has existed. The old general store that sold everything from penny candy to shotgun shells has evolved into the one-stop big boxes of Wal-Mart and Target. Companies like Starbucks know that, although their public persona is that of a coffee retailer, their real mission is to create the ideal coffee drinking experience and sell their customers on an array of paraphernalia carrying the Starbucks brand—everything from T-shirts to mugs to compact discs, with the intent being to extend that experience well beyond the store. Once customers have a relationship with your brand, many opportunities to create incremental value for those same customers will emerge. Provided that the opportunities are consistent with your brand positioning and you deeply understand the emerging needs and wants of your target customers, you can create significant growth for your business.

However, it's taken most companies a long time to understand the value of what they already possess. Many companies spent the 1980s and early 1990s trying out fad strategy after fad strategy, seeking to pump up margins. Operational efficiency techniques such as total quality management, reengineering, and enterprise resource planning sounded good to investors and upper management, but in many cases they ended up being just different ways of rearranging deck chairs on the *Titanic.*

Then came the mid-1990s, when companies started looking at their top lines and focusing on tracking and analyzing key customer and transaction data. These companies began drinking deep from the cup of customer relationship management, streamlining customer service procedures and training their call center staffs to field calls in new ways. They spent heavily on CRM installations, fully expecting that CRM would be the Holy Grail of profitability that ERP was not.

But in their infatuation with the new technology, they missed a fundamental truth about the limitations of that technology: The fastest car in the world won't get you anywhere if you don't know how to drive . . . or exactly where you want to go.

CRM AND CROSS-SELLING

In many industries and companies today, the terms *customer relationship management* and *cross-selling* are frequently used interchangeably. For instance, financial institutions focused on cross-selling multiple products to their customers will measure their success in terms of the number of "relationships" that they have built with the customer, with each relationship representing a different product that has been sold. To be sure, CRM has its uses in enabling cross-sell initiatives. Given the wealth of data about customers that CRM is capable of tracking, it makes sense that these systems would be used to reveal opportunities to build a productive, profitable brand experience (and thereby justify their existence). Applied properly, CRM can make the sales, marketing, and service organizations within a company run more smoothly, keeping the focus on the customer's needs and wants—often before the customer is even aware of them.

However, as discussed in Chapter 5, the majority of CRM applications are either misapplied or misused. Berkeley Enterprise Partners estimates that a full *70 percent* of CRM projects do not produce measurable business benefits. The reasons are myriad—inappropriate tools, inability to take action, inadequate corporate structures— but they all boil down to a single core mistake: the failure to use a brand architecture and the desired brand experience for customers to inform the design and implementation of CRM technologies enablers. Bringing a variety of expensive customer relationship management systems online is foolish if you're not using them in conjunction with a tightly focused, targeted, data driven series of strategic steps aimed at creating a productive, profitable brand experience for your customers.

While companies have taken the necessary and critical step of investing in technology and analyzing customer data, many have not thought through the strategic brand implications of focusing on customer retention and relationships. They may now be able to cross-sell, but they are not cross-marketing. You may get lucky enough to sell someone a couple of ancillary or related products, but without a coherent strategy, that's just a happy accident, not a measurable, repeatable action.

BEFORE YOU CAN CROSS-SELL, YOU HAVE TO CROSS-MARKET

So the secret, then, is not just keeping customers locked in your store, so to speak, until they relent and buy something. The goal is to develop a marketing strategy that activates customer intent to cross-buy from you. You can use enabling technologies to determine what they're buying, why they're buying it, what you must say to get them to buy more, and how to tailor other existing or potential products to meet their conscious and unconscious needs.

Contrary to the beliefs (or desires) of some marketers, customers aren't lemmings, willing to follow companies anywhere they lead. If a bank tries to cross-sell a credit card to a customer just because the customer happens to be applying for an auto loan without first developing a cohesive strategy to offer compelling benefits, then the customer just won't buy it. Worse, he or she may get annoyed with the experience and choose not to do business with that bank at all. Companies will not be effective in cross-selling bundles of products to new customers, nor reap the real results of selling more products to their current customers, until they fully understand the needs, wants, and motivations of their customers—and, most important, how these relate to the benefits offered by the brand. They must shift perspective from an inside-out focus on a sale and execution of a transaction to marketing a set of benefits to enhance the customer's life and relationship with the company's brand.

Cross-selling, by definition, is driven by business unit level or sales representative tactics. From the customers' perspective, this may be presented as a laundry list of products that may or may not be connected to any meaningful benefits for them. The offers are typically presented in a context that may be difficult for a customer to understand (e.g., "Just help me refinance my mortgage so I can lower my monthly payment; I don't know what this home equity line thing is!").

By contrast, cross-marketing is driven by a customer-centric approach whereby customers see individual products in the context of specific benefits to them and an overarching brand experience with your company (e.g., "I understand that after I refinance, I have significant equity in my house. It would make sense to secure a home equity line that I can tap into as I need additional funds to renovate my kitchen."). Obviously, to cross-market effectively, you need much more information about customers and their specific needs at the moment of truth. (See Figure 6.1.)

As with any bleak picture, there's always a brighter side. The companies that are able to shift their focus and understand that they're responsible for a brand experience over and above a product will reap the benefits of loyal customers many times over.

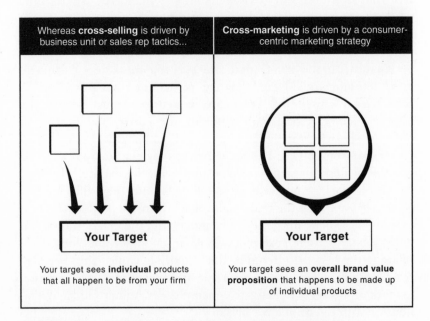

FIGURE 6.1   From Cross-Selling to Cross-Marketing

THE PROMISE OF CROSS-MARKETING
TECHNOLOGIES

Fortunately for corporations seeking to embrace a cross-marketing approach, the tools that can move marketing to the next level are widely available and highly configurable. With these tools, companies can develop comprehensive plans to address their existing markets, create deep and extended relationships with current customers, and identify unseen and unused marketing opportunities—in short, cross-market in the most meaningful and profitable sense of the word.

For instance, Zyman Marketing Group uses a data-rich analysis tool called the Return on Marketing Investment (ROMI) model (more about this in Chapter 9), which permits analysis of the historical performance of marketing channels; projects the levels of prospects, lead meetings, and wins that will be necessary to meet prescribed revenue targets; and develops monthly lead requirements and forecasts to evaluate progress against business goals. With such a tool, companies can keep constant track of how well their cross-marketing efforts are working, analyzing potential areas for improvement and reengineering.

On a broader scale, enterprise marketing management fuels the most ambitious and successful cross-marketing efforts. For instance, marketing process reengineering, the management of increasingly complex marketing channels, rests at the heart of cross-marketing efforts. EMM applications can aid in the planning, execution, and measurement of marketing activities. The most efficient EMM applications combine intellectual capital associated with marketing processes and expertise with built-in organizational knowledge-capture capabilities.

At present, early-stage adopters and developers of EMM applications and technologies use the capabilities mostly to help manage the development of marketing program content, automate work flow, and integrate some applications. But before long, companies will adopt and implement EMM on a grand scale, giving them the ability to strategically plan, coordinate, and measure all the impacts of their internal and external marketing efforts.

EMM applications can help marketers make better marketing decisions while decreasing marketing execution costs and reducing the time needed to bring ideas from the drawing board right to customers. And higher productivity means marketers will spend less time thinking about lower-level activities and more time on in-depth analysis, strategic thinking, creative efforts, and other higher-value activities.

POSSIBLE PITFALLS OF CROSS-MARKETING

It all seems so easy, doesn't it? Bring some brand and marketing strategies and some new technologies to the table, and your customers willingly enter into an endless loop of purchases, continually generating income for you and satisfaction for them. What could be simpler?

Naturally, cross-marketing does have its share of pitfalls, and corporations must acknowledge the risks. Chief among these is the burden of expectation. As connections with and commitments to customers deepen, the customers in turn expect an exponentially greater level of satisfaction from the company. The more companies promise and the more they actually provide to customers, the more customers will want and expect them to provide. The bar is constantly being raised. But if corporations fail to perform to expectations, they risk squandering years of goodwill built up by intensive cross-marketing efforts. All the technology and strategy in the world isn't going to help a company that's not ready to serve its customers when needed.

BREADTH AND DEPTH

The key to cross-marketing is broadening the definition of markets in which you compete and deepening the meaning of your brand—both for customers and for the company itself. For instance, a traditional tax preparer such as H&R Block can increase its market share and share of wallet among customers by redefining its market by, say, positioning itself as a "leading provider of financial advice services," offering tax advice, investment advice, and home mortgage services for its customers. In doing so, H&R Block is well positioned to cross-market a wide variety of advice products to ensure the financial health and well-being of their customers. At the same time, they can lock down profitable, recurring, long-term relationships with those same customers as their financial services partner of choice. Using a combination of technological analysis and strategic benchmarking, companies can create measurable, achievable goals for bringing their customers back, time and time again.

Cross-marketing carries many risks, but the reward is the most prized asset of any company: a productive, profitable relationship with a loyal, repeat customer.

CASE STUDY: Wells Fargo

CROSS-MARKETING TO INCREASE RELATIONSHIPS PER CUSTOMER

Formed in 1852, the financial services firm Wells Fargo Inc. has $312 billion in assets, including 5,400 stores and 6,400 ATMs across the United States. With a market cap of $84 billion and 134,000 employees, Wells Fargo reaches into 20 million households. Wells Fargo has thrived because it's been able to aggressively cross-market those households, selling a variety of services to each of its customers.

The company operates more than 330 subsidiaries in such fields as consumer and business banking services, investment services and products, venture capital investing, and international trade services. But the big moneymaker for Wells Fargo continues to be retail banking, which generates 42 percent of the company's annual revenue, primarily through private loans.

Wells Fargo has gone out of its way to connect with its customers in an attempt to close the gap with industry leader Bank of America. Customers have indicated that the Wells Fargo brand stands for security, trust, dependability, speed, and convenience, and Wells Fargo has tried to reward its customers by appealing to them on every level possible.

"We still deliver timely information to our customers every day," says Wells Fargo CEO Dick Kovacevich. "In 1890, it was via the Wells Fargo Pony Express; today it is via Wells Fargo online."

As part of its long-term strategic plan, Wells Fargo has decided to increase its service relationships per customer. Most financial institutions have about 1.5 relationships per customer, including checking accounts, savings accounts, home equity loans, and so forth. By comparison, Wells Fargo has 3.8 relationships and plans to increase that to 8.0 relationships through aggressive cross-marketing efforts.

Some of these efforts include plans to put a Wells Fargo credit and debit card in every wallet; credit cards are now used by 23.1 percent of Wells Fargo's customers, up from 21.2 percent in 2000. Debit cards are up to 83 percent from 59 percent three years ago. Wells Fargo is working to match the service needs of its customers. On the higher end, Wells Fargo is working to keep its higher-value customers, each of whom typically carries an average of 7.3 products. The company is working to leverage its key acquisitions in this arena, including Conseco Finance, ACO Brokerage, Acordia Insurance, and HD Vest. Wells Fargo also wants to achieve a 100 percent cross-sell rate for its bank, mortgage, and home equity loans.

Cross-marketing doesn't work if you don't have customers willing to pay attention to your offerings, and Wells Fargo is working to deliver outstanding sales and service to every customer, providing advice and guidance as a prelude to cross-selling. Wells Fargo bases its cross-marketing efforts on the individual customer's situation and specific needs, wants, and motivations. Taking into account its customers' life stages, financial resources, and changing needs, Wells Fargo organizes its cross-marketing programs based on the way different customers buy and use financial service products.

Wells Fargo's stated goal is to support its customers from cradle to grave, so to speak. Initiatives include a "Banking on Our Future" program introducing financial basics to children; on the other end of the spectrum is a complete suite of retirement planning and management services.

Wells Fargo has a comprehensive plan in place for capturing information on its customers. Every mortgage application provides an in-depth look at customer needs and financial resources. A Homeowners' Pack bundles checking, credit cards, and a home equity loan into a single offering. And Wells Fargo's e-bank software retains and links customer data. On the internal side, cross-marketing targets are built into operating budgets and performance goals, providing for increased accountability and commitment throughout the organization.

In short, Wells Fargo has cracked the code on cross-marketing, realizing that cross-selling, by its very definition, is not customer-centric. Lines of business mean nothing to customers, so Wells Fargo decided to cross-market to customers based on the way that they purchase rather than the way the company is organized. The benefits are apparent for both sides: Customers see better pricing on products and time savings

with one-stop shopping, while Wells Fargo enjoys higher customer retention rates and increased profitability and shareholder returns.

MARKETER'S SCIENTIFIC METHOD: CROSS-MARKET TO CROSS-SELL

Fortunately, most companies understand the value of cross-selling
and the capabilities of CRM technologies; the key now is to get them
to work together. In order to build on their cross-selling capabilities
and transform these assets into cross-marketing successes, companies
need to alter their mind-sets, and even their corporate structures, to
take advantage of the potential for cross-marketing to customers.

Step 1: Always Start with a Deep Understanding of the Customer

Base cross-marketing efforts on the individual customer's situation
and specific needs, wants, motivations, and purchase occasions.

- ~ Consider customer factors such as life stage, current and
  future financial resources, changing needs, and channel
  preferences and capabilities (e.g., Internet access, wireless usage) for service and support.
- ~ Recognize that the way you talk about, organize, and run
  your company means nothing to your customers—you
  must speak their language and organize around their
  needs.
- ~ Organize your cross-marketing programs based on the
  way different customers buy and use your products and
  services.
- ~ Analyze the specific occasions on which your products and
  services are purchased or consumed, and hypothesize reasons for additional consumption on that particular occasion or ways to create new occasions for consumption.
- ~ Create products and services to support customers from
  cradle to grave—anticipating future needs and evolving
  offers to mirror evolving need sets.

Step 2: Align Everyone That Speaks with Customers

When it comes to cross-marketing, nobody stays on the sidelines. Companies must initiate tighter integrations with their marketing partners, including promotion agencies, ad agencies, public relations, and vendors, so that cross-marketing execution is consistent with strategy.

Step 3: Measure Results and Debrief Successes and Failures

Companies must monitor cross-marketing results and quantify new knowledge and improvements on a frequent, continuous basis. This information must be matched and tracked against a series of corporate goals, expectations, and milestones in order to keep on track. Sometimes debriefing the successes (Why did this program work so well? How can we do more of it?) is more important than analyzing the failures.

The most important tenet to remember about cross-marketing is that it's all about brand and the relationships that your customers form with your brand. Brand and marketing strategy must come front and center, form and inform the connections attempted with consumers and the relationships developed over time.

7

USE NEW MEDIA FOR

BRAND ACTIVATION

Imagine, for a moment, that it's 1999 again. The dot-com revolution isn't a bubble, it's an elevator with only one direction. Everybody's rich, everybody's happy, every marketing decision is a stroke of brilliance, right?

Now return to today. After the dot-com bubble burst, the truth about the Internet revolution became clear amid the ruins of destroyed portfolios, shattered careers, and horrific spending levels dressed up as marketing. The Internet revolution had done more harm to the notion of a new science of marketing than could have been imagined.

The so-called great marketing of the day was nothing more than gambling. When you win the lottery with your venture capital firm, you turn around, put your money on red, and roll the dice. In this case, the dice were anything from obtuse or absurd television commercials to crazy PR stunts. Newly anointed zillionaire CEOs would proudly announce that they were spending $40 million *creating* their brand, using everything from trinkets and trash to people dressed up in chicken suits parading around American cities.

Thankfully, that era is over, leaving everyone poorer but smarter. The enduring lesson of the dot-com revolution is that "eyeballs" do indeed matter—but only when they're connected to a brain that tells the hand to pull out a wallet and make a purchase. Otherwise, they're not worth the time you've spent trying to capture them.

Even though the Internet bubble caused a collective cringe among real marketers worldwide, it wasn't entirely without merit. It helped engender the development of a superb new marketing tool for managing a brand experience and tying together disparate elements of marketing. The new media utterly changed the science of marketing as we know it.

First things first—what are new media? They are all of the tools of the *electronic channel* used to communicate with and engage current and prospective customers. This definition includes the Internet, web sites, e-mail, instant messaging, online services, cell phones, and PDAs, among many other forms of media. In their most basic form, new media deliver the ability to engage in an *electronic conversation* with customers, wherever they may be. This electronic conversation can take place at whatever stage the customer may be in the brand experience—considering needs, using a product, waiting for service, or any other point.

Suffice it to say that the new media present a marketing opportunity unparalleled in history. Never before has it been possible to manage your brand experience by using such an intimate, ongoing conversation with your customer.

Certainly, companies have communicated electronically for decades. But tools such as electronic data interchange (EDI) were historically used only to ship data files between two computers. That's not what most people would consider a conversation, and it certainly can't deliver much in the way of a brand's benefits.

All of this doesn't even touch on the most beneficial trait of new media—in most cases, they are incredibly cheap. When you compare the cost of preparing and delivering an e-mail against the cost of nearly any other media (consumer promotion, call center support, billboards, print, radio, or TV), new media will invariably win on the efficiency scale. While new media make managing a brand experience possible, you simply can't leave it to chance that sales or service or operations will get it right when it comes to communicating and delivering those brand benefits that you know will drive purchase intent.

Marketing must play a significant role—and here's why. Because the other parts of the organization look on working with the customer as something of a chore, and because new media are rapidly becoming the primary communication vehicle for all of these areas (e.g., invoice confirmations are sent as e-mails these days), marketing has an opportunity to use its mastery of new media to mastermind all communication across all customer touch points. As the electronic conversation increasingly becomes the primary conversation with customers, marketing has an opportunity to exert itself as the primary owner of that conversation. Marketing can ensure that all of the benefits of the brand are communicated clearly, consistently, and compellingly, regardless of the customer touch point or interaction.

There's no more time to waste—the time is *now* for you to assert your role as a marketer and to use new media to make that role possible.

But just as you didn't learn how to use e-mail by simply turning on your computer, you can't expect new media to work for you as soon as you flip the switch. Putting new media to work requires the following steps:

1. Development of a brand architecture that articulates the combination of attributes, functional benefits, and emotional benefits that drive purchase intent.
2. Establishment of the brand's character or personality. This will come into play once you decide to execute a marketing program and need to answer questions about such elements as the tone of your communication— serious, whimsical, smarmy, or some other approach. The brand's personality provides a description of the brand in human terms. This description establishes the overall tone for marketing executions.
3. Definition of the elements of the brand experience and creation of a brand experience blueprint. The brand experience blueprint must take into account the multiple channels that a customer might use to interact with your company. For example, if your customers interact with you via a distributor, then you must build the presence of this distributor into the model.

    The brand experience blueprint should take new media into account when planning for specific customer outcomes. These outcomes are the behaviors that you would like for your customers to emulate. They can be anything from downloading a brochure when they begin to consider a purchase to enrollment in an e-mail-based service newsletter. These outcomes must be measurable and must include traditional financial metrics, such as revenue, volume, profit, and cash flow.

4. Evaluate, once the blueprint is in place, how you might continue to integrate new media (web sites, e-mail, instant messaging, and so on) to further segment customers by behavior and continue to deliver those benefits that you know drive purchase intent.

For many companies, especially those in industrial or business-to-business sectors, this sort of electronic communication is the lion's share of any customer communication. The electronic channel tends to be the most efficient vehicle for companies to communicate with each other, across all departments—from engineer to engineer, from purchasing agent to salesperson. Unfortunately, these same companies are the ones most likely to think of marketing's responsibilities as limited to corporate communications (i.e., press releases) or annual reports. The same companies that are the most likely to derive the benefits from putting new media to work seem to be the furthest behind in imagining how this approach can communicate and deliver on brand benefits to targeted segments.

Despite the compelling benefits of new media, many companies are still behind the curve when it comes to putting them to their best use. When you combine the ability to engage in a one-on-one conversation with your customers with remarkably compelling cost advantages, what could possibly stand in the way of making new media the centerpiece of every marketing effort under way today?

In addition to the general economic conditions, the "head in the sand" mentality, and resistance to experimentation, big companies cite several reasons for avoiding the adoption of new media.

We Don't Know with Whom to Speak

A life history of not using new media means that a company simply doesn't *have the e-mail addresses* of its customers or prospects. For mass marketers, up until recently, the value of creating an extensive database of customers was questionable. But now it's an imperative for *every* company. The math is excruciatingly simple. Your company will simply not be well placed to compete in the future if you don't start *right now* gathering the e-mail addresses (and electronic conversation habits) of your current customers and prospects.

In addition to not knowing the e-mail addresses, many companies aren't really sure of their customers' needs. In industrial examples, the purchasing agent who actually executes the sale could be a world apart from the engineer who has to use your product to create another finished good. New media represent an ideal vehicle for reaching out, economically and electronically, and delivering your brand benefits to ensure that you're marketing correctly at each stage of the brand experience.

We Don't Know What to Say

It's hard enough to get one message right. Very few companies are organized or prepared for delivering highly customized messages—that is, actually engaging in a lively conversation—across all possible customer touch points and all marketing communications and media vehicles. The required level of capability doesn't exist in most companies today.

EMM requires that the brand architecture be applied across every stage of the brand experience. However, the traditional messaging generated by the brand architecture is entirely too narrow. While it's important that the brand architecture should form the heart of any and all messages and conversations, most companies have yet to think through all of the potential conversations they might have—and what benefits can build the greatest customer value. For example, how should the company communicate with lapsed customers—those who have purchased one product or service but have never come back to the brand for more? How should the elements of the brand architecture be translated to address reenlisting someone in the brand franchise? These are just a few of the questions that must be addressed in the brand experience blueprint.

We Don't Know What's Possible to Do

The historical corporate gap of understanding between marketers and information technologists has left most marketers unable to even conceive of how to put new media to work. There's very little experimentation in this area, even though it's inexpensive to do so. Just understanding how elements like a database work is so unfamiliar to marketers that they don't even venture into discovering ways to use an electronic conversation with their customers and their prospects to drive more sales.

The most sophisticated marketing techniques will forever lie beyond the grasp of marketers who continue to market as if it were the twentieth century and not the twenty-first. The key to understanding what you need to do is, first and foremost, determine what you *want* to happen. Consider: What is your destination for the brand experience? What are the desired outcomes at each stage? Broken down further, what are the potential scenarios at each stage of the brand experience and how are you going to communicate your brand's benefits within those scenarios? Again, these questions are part of developing a brand experience blueprint.

Once scientific marketers have a grasp of this customer-centric perspective, they can use the brand experience blueprint to identify potential fixes or combinations of content and functionality that will address the gap between where they are and where they want to be.

We Don't Know What or How to Measure Results

When new media first became available, companies initially used them to focus on simply attracting eyeballs to a site. This is the equivalent of evaluating advertising by focusing on awareness; it's not very useful. Just because customers are *aware* of your brand, that doesn't necessarily mean that awareness will translate into any kind of purchase.

While purchases are important, marketers need to count more than sales dollars. Each stage in the brand experience can be measured, usually by identifying those specific customer outcomes or behaviors that you would like for your customer to experience. For example, if your customer comes to your web site for the first time ever and is considering your company or your set of products and services, what do you as a marketer want that customer to do? Do you know?

The desired customer outcomes are just that—if you could design the brand experience at a certain stage, what would that be? The power of new media is that once you have designed that brand experience, you have the power to determine whether it's actually driving customers to buy more stuff. The key to selling more is making sure your customers know exactly what you're offering—and it takes a lot more than just hanging out your shingle and saying something is available for sale.

THE NEW MEDIA HURDLE:
GET TO KNOW THE CUSTOMER

One irony of the emergence of new media as a powerful marketing tool is that it has actually put mass marketers on the defensive. The Procter & Gambles, the Coca-Colas, the Krafts of the world—veritable fortresses of marketing that spend billions of dollars trying to reach their consumers—are now in an awkward situation. They can't take full advantage of new media because they don't actually know the names of their customers or their e-mail addresses.

When the potential of one-to-one marketing became apparent, the traditional consumer marketers weren't really ready. They still remain far from the vanguard when it comes to putting new media to work.

The companies best positioned to put new media to work today are those that have built on a direct relationship with their customers. Companies like American Express, Blockbuster Entertainment, and even Microsoft and Apple are much further ahead. Companies that sell through a retailer or another party are at a distinct disadvantage.

What traditional brand marketers have been slow to catch on to is the fact that *new media make all media new again.* The advent of new media makes it inexpensive to include a call to action on literally every piece of communication delivered. That call to action could be as simple as a single tag line: "Learn more at Coke.com." What would have been an expensive exercise using a call center (say, 1-800-Get-COKE) that would be quite limited in what it could deliver—after all, what breadth of communication can you have via a customer service rep?—can now be replaced with a much more complete and interactive communication.

Companies that want to make the most of new media must integrate them into literally every element of the marketing mix. Consider it a lens that gives a marketer a view of the impact marketing is actually having on the customer. Every element of the marketing mix should be tracked and monitored at all times, which in turn makes closer tracking of consumer behavior a possibility.

The role of the marketer is to build the database of customer knowledge over time, to gradually enable new media to be better integrated with many other elements of the marketing mix.

New media can also aid business marketers. While business marketers may have the addresses of the buyers of their products, most of them still haven't taken the critical step of creating a profile, centered on an e-mail address, of all of the potential players in the overall brand experience between the two companies. EMM requires that the compelling brand benefits drive communications or a conversation across all customer touch points. In many instances, especially for corporate purchases, the buyer of the product is not the user of the product.

Taking up our prior example of ACME packaging, a hypothetical supplier to Nabisco, ACME might work very closely with Nabisco's purchasing department to close the deal. However, building the brand experience extends outward both ways from the purchase—upstream to the prepurchase period and downstream to after-purchase support. If ACME uses new media to build the brand experience, then the critical communication will begin with the true decision makers upstream, including the package designers and the bakery engineers responsible for producing the cookies & crackers. Downstream, communication will include the Nabisco marketers and salespeople, who are in turn responsible for managing *their* brand experience with the consumer. New media give business-to-business marketers the power to communicate brand benefits across every key touch point and offer the opportunity to escape the "you're selling a commodity" trap and build more value into their products and relationships.

For most companies, the critical difficulty isn't getting their hands on e-mail addresses. The issue is figuring out what to do once those addresses are available and those relationships are built. Most marketers are smart enough to leverage all existing media to build an extensive and up-to-date database of their customers. The problem is, up to this point, the lack of a coherent objective has kept such organizational management from happening. If you haven't started, start today—because now you have an idea of what you might say and why you would want to say it.

LET'S GIVE THEM SOMETHING TO TALK ABOUT

It's a significant challenge just to provide sales with a highly targeted message to speak directly to buyers. It's a rare marketing department indeed in corporate America that possesses all of the messaging needed to speak to every customer touch point at every stage of the brand experience. These companies can convert the brand architecture, as well as all associated emotional and functional benefits, into appropriate messaging. These messages are then delivered using new media, of course.

The key to translating the brand architecture into an engaging electronic conversation is the development of an understanding of the customer scenarios that are appropriate for that particular touch point, part of creating a brand experience blueprint. Continuing with the ACME and Nabisco example, a critical step in putting new media to work across the brand experience is to break down the potential conversation into its component parts.

YOU CAN'T WIN UNLESS YOU CAN SEE WHAT NEW MEDIA MAKE POSSIBLE

While it's nearly impossible to miss examples of new media being put to use in the more traditional domain of marketing communication (for instance, the dreaded e-mailbox of spam), what hasn't been covered in great detail are those opportunities for putting new media to work across all of the elements of the brand experience. Marketers enjoy an unprecedented ability to leverage low-cost new media to create, build, and maintain a lifetime relationship with a customer, without requiring any physical interaction with that customer.

The beauty of new media is that the efficacy of any of these concepts is easily measurable—provided you establish measurement parameters in the development of the concept. For example, a Web-based cholesterol monitoring tool might be an enjoyable perk, but it's worthless if no one is using it, and it's almost equally worthless if it can't be shown that use of the monitoring delivers more patients who stay on their medication. The name of the game is delivering on customer outcomes and *also* delivering on brand benefits.

HOW DO NEW MEDIA MEASURE UP?

New media have come a long way in a very short time. At its intro-duction, the concept of "eyeballs"—simple views of a given site or content selection—was the limit of what was measurable. Today's software can provide most marketers with more information than they can actually use. So what should marketers be measuring with new media?

For any new media investment, the overarching concern is return on investment. Given that many marketers aren't even thinking about ROI—and would have a challenge ahead of them if they did (think billboards)—new media is a welcome change.

Return on investment for new media tends to come from a number of different sources:

~ **Sales of the same stuff:**   For those companies that are executing transactions using a web site or some other new media–driven vehicle, this is an easily attainable metric. Many companies look to new media as their new channel for selling their existing product or service set.

~ **Cost reduction:**   An alternative return might come from the reduced cost of servicing existing customers. The cost to serve a banking customer via a web site is dramatically lower—and, in many instances, better—than the cost of maintaining branches filled with tellers. This reduction of cost to serve might be an element of your return on investment.

~ **Customer retention:**   You may be able to use new media to show that your efforts to build a brand experi-ence have actually reduced the churn of existing cus-tomers. Put another way, you have used new media to increase customer retention. The end result is more sales and, possibly, reduced spending on traditional media or direct selling. For nearly every company, it's remarkably more efficient to sell more to your current customers than to try to find that elusive new customer.

~ **Sales of new stuff:**   This is where worlds are opening up. The smartest companies are figuring out how new media provide previously unimagined opportunities for creating and selling new combinations of products and services. General Electric serves as an excellent example of this new opportunism. Before the advent of new media, GE Medical earned the lion's share of its revenues selling products.

Over the past several years, the share of product revenue has dropped dramatically and the share of service revenue has skyrocketed. Even more appealing is the fact that service revenue carries higher margins against the cutthroat competition on products. So how is this possible? GE realized that using new media to provide ongoing services, software updates, and maintenance on a long-term, contract basis was a far more profitable business for the medical division. Much as the latest versions of Microsoft Windows and Apple OS X (and many other software packages) include automatic updates, GE realized that these updates could solidify the brand experience, smooth out revenues over time, and also lead to higher margins. As an added bonus, the service level for GE Medical's customers improved dramatically. GE is on top of any maintenance problems, sometimes before its customers are even aware of them.

~ **Achievement/optimization of customer outcomes:** On a more basic level, marketers need to understand not only what is selling, but also what actually makes sales happen. Part of bringing a scientific approach to marketing is experimenting with all of the different levers that might improve sales. New media can be evaluated based on their ability to achieve desired customer outcomes. If you have learned that 25 percent of the people who receive a certain coupon or offer will walk into your retail store and buy something, then you can simply measure the ability to deliver these offers. What are you going to put in place—what content, what functionality—to drive people to download that offer and get them to bring it into a retail store?

Alternately, it may be just as important to use new media to keep customers engaged in your business. If you're Blockbuster, you may want to measure the power of new media to drive traffic into your stores or, more specifically, use new media to drive incremental visits.

Or you might use differing levels of new media to drive traffic, based on what you know about the behavior of your customers. At what point do people fall out of the purchase cycle and need that extra push to get them back into the cycle? While Blockbuster has a short cycle, companies like Disney, with its theme parks, have a much longer cycle. Disney might measure the power of new media to shorten the cycle between Disney World visits, not just the sale of stuffed Winnie the Pooh dolls.

So how do you measure these outcomes? The advantage of new media is that nearly everything that every customer does is recorded at some point. The challenge—and granted, it's a good problem to have—is that you'll end up with reams of data. Software vendors today can give marketers the ability to track specific customer outcomes and then adjust efforts and campaigns accordingly.

For example, many companies today look at new media metrics that resemble the graph in Figure 7.1. It's no wonder that marketing gave up on measuring campaigns with metrics like these. How can you tell what on earth is going on? Part of the problem for many companies is that they haven't actually designed their new media efforts around desired outcomes, so the metrics aren't really clear either. They *can't* be.

New measurement software will let marketers see what customers are actually doing when they interact with new media. Con-

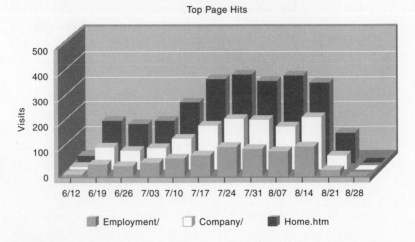

Top Page Hits

Visits

0   100   200   300   400   500

6/12 6/19 6/26 7/03 7/10 7/17 7/24 7/31 8/07 8/14 8/21 8/28

Employment/   Company/   Home.htm

FIGURE 7.1   The Meaninglessness of Measuring Page Hits

sider again the Nabisco/ACME example: A marketer dedicated to building ACME's brand experience for Nabisco will want to know whether he or she is (1) achieving desired customer outcomes and (2) understanding correctly the behavior of his or her target at this stage of the brand experience—to wit, the bakery engineer. What are packaging designers doing when they interact with ACME? Are marketing's assumptions correct about how Nabisco likes to interact with ACME's new media resources?

To get at customer outcomes, marketers have to get down in the trenches and measure such outcomes. Fortunately, the software now exists that will provide images of the actual behavior of customers, which can let you know whether they're doing what you thought they would do and give you the opportunity to make alterations if necessary. Figure 7.2 is an example from a company named

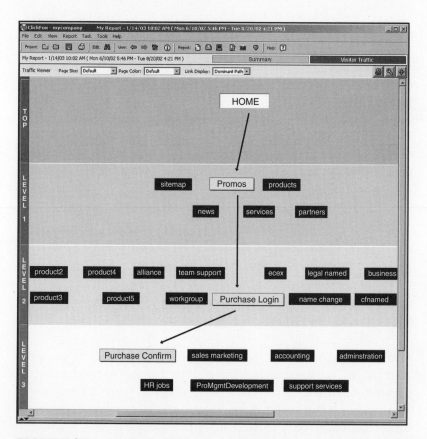

FIGURE 7.2   Analyzing Customer Behavior to Reveal Insight

ClickFox. By evaluating these customer behaviors, marketers can get real insight into whether their new media investments are generating the brand results that are required.

Results are only as good as the questions asked of the data. Superficial questions yield superficial returns. Why not ask your IT department to give you an idea of what your customers are doing, rather than just showing you how many people might have visited your company web site?

YOUR SECRET WEAPON

New media represent the most compelling way to experiment as a marketer. Every company can benefit from rolling up its sleeves and experimenting with how to use new media to drive profitable sales, deliver on the benefits articulated in the brand architecture, and achieve desired customer outcomes for every scenario. It's almost unthinkable to try to manage a brand experience without new media.

Marketers need to expand their notions of new media beyond the notion that it's anything like a print ad, a TV ad, or a coupon. Instead, they need to think about how new media can be the secret weapon that lets them manage and take ownership of the brand experience. Whether you're ACME working with Nabisco on a billion-dollar relationship or you're selling bumper stickers out of your basement, you can always use new media to drive your business to new heights.

CASE STUDY: M&M's

USING NEW MEDIA PROMOTIONS TO ACTIVATE PURCHASE INTENT

M&M's, the candy-coated chocolate that "melts in your mouth, not in your hands," is manufactured and globally distributed by Mars Incorporated. According to company folklore, it was Forrest Mars, son of founder Frank Mars, who came up with the idea to give chocolate a protective candy coat to stop it from melting. He was working in Europe during the 1930s and identified the need for a convenient snack that could be transported easily and traveled well in a variety of climates. That idea became M&M's candies—more than 400 million of which are produced each day, totaling more than 146 billion each year. Today, Mars Inc. is a truly global business and M&M's are famous worldwide. The company continues to be known in the market for innovation and manufactures many leading brands within the snack category, including Snickers, Mars, and Twix.

Consistent with their heritage of innovation, Mars has been one of the leaders in using Internet marketing and new media to market their products and build online communities to connect with their target audience. There are several sites that the company supports for each entry into the snack foods category. For M&M's there are at least three unique sites:

- www.mms.com—a distinctive web site that serves as the portal to many of the other sites that support the M&M's brand. The site cleverly highlights M&M's sponsorship of NASCAR racing and gives youth a chance to interact with driver Ken Schrader and the M&M's Racing Team. The M&M's site is frequently updated, and completely redesigned on a regular basis—although it always retains its core content sections. There is an online shop that sells M&M's and associated products. However, the main purpose of the site is to promote interest in M&M's with colorful, highly interactive, and very entertaining content. The site also recognizes that M&M's are sold around the world, so there are country buttons for at least the most significant M&M's markets. M&M's have operated this web site over several years, and it is now a very sophisticated and successful example of online marketing.
- www.marsbrightideas.com—This site appears to be targeting moms and dads more than the kids. It is an online community, hosted by M&M's "spokescandies" Red and Yellow, that delivers useful information for parents on how to use the product in baking, recipes of kids' favorites, decorating ideas, family fun activities, and other many other tips for how to get the most out of the "M&M's experience." Visitors are encouraged to join the community and enter their own holiday recipe ideas, family activity or cute craft idea, and they are given a cash incentive to do so. Besides M&M's, many of Mars's other snack food category entrants are featured on the site, including Snickers, Starburst, Dove, and Skittles.

Interestingly, the site is organized around seasons and special events—consumption occasions when Mars products can be used to enhance the overall family experience.

- www.colorworks.com—This innovative site appears to be the real engine for driving sales of M&M's online. In this case, the site is targeting a much broader audience beyond their core youth market. Consumers can customize the collection of colors that they would like to have in their own personalized batch of M&M's—picking from 21 available colors to assemble their own bag of treats. For those who need a little inspiration there are preselected combinations such as team-spirit school colors (University of Virginia: dark blue and orange), special color combinations (e.g., Patriotic: red, white, and blue), seasonal colors (e.g., Autumn Hay Ride: yellow, gold, cream), special occasion colors (e.g., "It's a Boy": blue and white), even corporate colors to be used at the next corporate golf outing or given away as promotional pieces. The M&M's colorworks site also features a simple affiliate program that allows other companies to add links, banners, buttons, or even an entire online store to their company web site as a way to enhance the company site and earn commissions on whatever their visitors buy on the M&M's site after they click through the links.

M&M's serves as an excellent example to emulate when considering how to put new media to work at selling more products. The M&M's brand has a distinct brand architecture that articulates the combination of product attributes (e.g., "sweet milk chocolate with a candy crunch"), functional benefits (e.g., "melts in you mouth—not in your hand"), and emotional benefits (e.g., "fun, family-enriching experiences") that drive purchase intent. Over the years, M&M's has established the brand's character and personality by executing marketing programs featuring their "spokescandies." As such, the brand has taken on a personality in human terms: Red, the wise-cracking, know-it-all chocolate on your pillow; Yellow, the nice guy in touch with his inner child; and Green, the feminine heroine who "melts for no one"; and so forth. Furthermore, Mars understands they must continuously define the experience that consumers have with the M&M's brand. They take into account the multiple channels that a consumer might use to interact with the brand, identify purchase influencers (e.g., parents) in the decision-making process, and plan for the specific consumption occasions (special occasions, team sporting events, etc.) that may occur across the brand experience. Now that Mars has all of these elements in place, they have been able to use new media (web sites, e-mail, instant messaging, and so on) to enhance the consumers' experience with the M&M's brand even further and deliver the specific brand messages that they know drive purchase intent. There is no better example of this than what Mars was able to achieve with the M&M's Global Color Vote in 2002.

Global Color Vote

The most ambitious effort undertaken in recent years has been M&M's Global Color Vote promotion. Essentially, Mars created a promotion to conduct an online global vote to determine the next new color of M&M's to be added to the colorful mix of chocolate candies. The M&M's Global Color Vote had to be positioned as different from all other consumer promotions—in scope, tonality, imagery, and execution—in order to signal its significance to the world while still maintaining the brand's positioning of "colorful chocolate fun." A comprehensive media relations campaign announced the Global Color Vote in the United States. Tactics included an advance to the Associated Press, B-roll distribution, and the creation of an online news bureau. A second announcement was made on March 6, 2002—poll opening day—featuring a live animation of M&M's "spokescandy": Red. In addition to building buzz around the brand, Mars was also aiming to see some immediate sales as a result of the campaign. Mars's thinking was that consumers—perhaps looking to inform themselves about the candidates prior to voting—would purchase specially marked M&M's packages containing the new candy colors.

And the Winner is . . .

The program culminated with an event in New York City on June 19, 2002, to reveal the winning color: purple. More than 10 million people from over 200 countries cast their vote via phone, mail, and through the World Wide Web. After months of sampling the choices in specially marked bags, the world chose purple, with 41 percent of the vote. Aqua received 38 percent of the vote, and pink garnered 19 percent of the vote. The remaining 2 percent of the vote went to various write-in colors. Beginning in August 2002, purple was to be added to the traditional blend of red, yellow, orange, green, blue, and brown

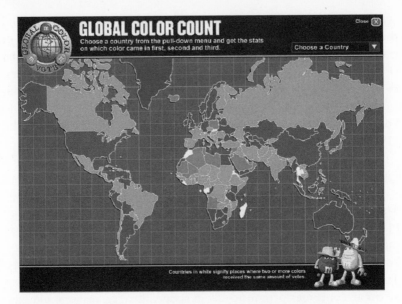

FIGURE 7.3   M&M's Global Color Vote Promotion

in M&M's bags. Figure 7.3 shows how the vote played out across the world. Detailed country-by-country statistics can be found at the official M&M's Global Vote Count web site (http://global.mms.com).

Results

The beauty of new media is that the efficacy of a promotion like M&M's Global Vote Count is easily measurable. Within three days of launching this online promotion, M&M's had achieved 1,250 placements and over 660 million impressions (an increase of over 170 percent), according to Nielsen/NetRatings. Traffic to the www.mms.com web site increased by 400 percent, and AOL welcome page hits generated over 600,000 votes in one day and more than 18,000 message board postings. Furthermore, the promotion successfully targeted the company's primary audience. The M&M's site attracted a predominantly female audience with a 67/33 gender split. "The recent online ad campaign by M&M's is a great case study in how Web advertising can leverage a strong brand, drive site traffic and enhance brand loyalty all in one fell swoop," said Charles Buchwalter, NetRatings vice president of media research. "M&M Mars scores twice by including the consuming public on the choice for a new color and also in receiving a significant boost in brand exposure." Most important, M&M's was able to enhance its leadership position as the largest candy brand in the world and maintain a highly profitable position in the $13 billion global snack foods category.

MARKETER'S SCIENTIFIC METHOD: USING NEW MEDIA FOR BRAND ACTIVATION

Following are the steps to follow in using new media to activate your brand.

Step 1: Identify the Stage of the Brand Experience

The first step is to understand who your customer might be at each stage of the brand experience. In many instances, there are multiple customers behind one purchase. Also, if possible, identify the brand preferences for these customers.

Step 2: Identify All Relevant Stakeholders/Customers

It's important not just to understand the role and position of your customers behind a purchase when preparing new media solutions. You need to have an idea of all stakeholders in the game—the suppliers, the manufacturers, the distributors, and all others involved in communicating and delivering on your brand benefits. Aligning these players ensures that you have consistent messaging no matter where your customer encounters your brand—which constitutes Step 3.

Step 3: Identify the Specific Touch Points That Are Currently Used for Each Customer

Each customer behind a purchase decision may interact with your company across multiple touch points. The next step is to understand your current customer behavior when it comes to interacting with your company. What have you "trained" your customers to do—call your sales rep, wait on hold at your call center, or send an email? Understanding the current customer touch points is critical to putting new media to work.

Step 4: Develop the Specific Scenarios for Customer Interaction at Each Stage of the Brand Experience

The next step is to determine specific scenarios for customer inter-action. Like all good marketing, this stage requires getting into the head of your customer. A bandwidth-heavy marketing campaign could annoy some of your online customers with slower connections; a contact-intensive campaign involving instant messaging and e-mailing could annoy your customers who prefer privacy. The key is to understand which customers prefer which means of interaction. Creating this sort of structural advantage in your go-to-market strat-egy inevitably leads to higher margins and many years of profitable sales thereafter.

Step 5: Craft the Elements of the Conversation

Once you've determined the proper methods of approaching each customer segment, you can craft the conversation to address the needs of each scenario, pulling from a mix of emotional benefits, functional benefits, and brand attributes developed in the brand architecture. It seems obvious that this kind of targeted market-ing works better than scattershot advertising or spamming, but a surprisingly large number of companies prefer to just throw their campaign funds in the air and hope they'll reach their proper cus-tomers. Targeting and focusing your message will inevitably lead to higher returns, since you're giving your customers exactly what they want.

Step 6: Develop the Mix of New Media That Delivers on the Identified Key Brand Benefits

Now that the scenario and the critical benefit have been identified, you can develop the new media content, concepts, and functionality than can best deliver the benefits. Is an interactive web site the best way to reach your customers? Direct e-mailing? Instant messaging? Or some combination of these and other new media? The opportu-nities to deliver your message are myriad; now it's just a matter of figuring out how to get your message into the right hands.

Strangely, one of the biggest challenges in developing the content across all stages of the brand experience is actually using the tools you already have. Most marketers have yet to embrace the power of new media, so in many cases it's become the burial ground for digital forms of all of the other media. It's relegated to little more than the library of the other media. That's like buying a brand-new Porsche and using only the CD player.

There's a lot of potential to use new media to speak directly to customers, no matter where they are. If your company is ever going to truly unlock all of its value, it has to realize that value lies inside the heads of your employees, not just in your products. Giving your best customers access to your great employees, and ideally selling them services, is the way that most of the product companies of the twentieth century have rapidly transformed themselves into the service companies of the twenty-first century.

PART III

Reinvent Your Business, Not Just Communications

8

RESTRUCTURE BASED
ON BRAND EXPERIENCE

Business leaders in virtually every industry face a common and recurring challenge: designing and maintaining effective and efficient business models that maximize profitability and return on marketing investment (ROMI) for their enterprise. While the quest for the optimal people, process, performance measures, and technology capabilities is hardly new, a collection of current forces—both internal and external—has forced the reinvention of business models across a wide spectrum of industries (see Figure 8.1).

Consider how the following drivers have impacted business models:

~ The globalization of competition
~ Decreased sustainability of competitive advantages due to technology innovations
~ Increasing demands from customers
~ Lowering of traditional barriers to entry and heightened demand for demonstrable returns on marketing investments

These changes have forced many companies to seek business model designs that yield the scale efficiencies of a centralized set

149

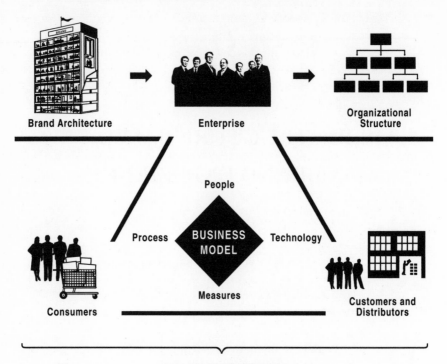

BRAND EXPERIENCE

FIGURE 8.1   Restructuring the Business Model

of capabilities, while still achieving the maximum effectiveness of close proximity to customers and consumers. Some enterprises are going even further, completely redefining how they build productive, profitable relationships across their extended enterprise, including suppliers, channel partners, customers, consumers, and, most important, their own people.

FORCING A REASSESSMENT OF BUSINESS MODEL DESIGN

Several key changes in the competitive environment over the past few years have necessitated a change in the way enterprises craft their business models:

~ **Increasing power of consumers.**   An unprecedented access to information about competing products, services, and pricing has given consumers more power than they've ever had before. Business leaders must make their current business designs more consumer-centric to meet and anticipate the needs and wants of their major constituencies.

~ **Increasing availability of high-quality information about customers.**   The other side of the coin is that, thanks to other technological advances, everyone across an enterprise can capture and mine extraordinary amounts of valuable customer and consumer data. In order to capitalize on the benefits of these consumer insights, many companies are reorganizing around key customer segments and centralizing common activities such as database marketing.

~ **Increasing demands of consolidated customers and channels.**   Across many industries, a few strong customers are concentrating and controlling buying power, placing suppliers increasingly at the mercy of customer and channel demands. Forward-thinking business leaders are taking these customers' specific needs into account by creating more customer-centric structures and developing targeted customer plans that treat these powerful customers and channel partners as priorities.

~ **Expansion into global markets.**   Trade liberalization and advances in communication technology have broken down traditional international barriers. Some companies are centralizing brand management and strategic planning to ensure consistent branding and marketing strategy across the globe, while others are capturing global economies of scale by centralizing activities such as media buying.

~ **Increasing financial scrutiny of marketing expenses.**   Marketing as a function is now being held to the same rigorous return on investment (ROI) standards as the rest of the enterprise. Rising spending and inadequate demonstration of marketing's ROI are drawing greater attention (and resistance) from the CEO's office and the finance department. In order to improve efficiency of marketing investments, many marketers are centralizing those activities that may benefit from scale economies, such as market research and media buying.

These forces are driving business leaders to reassess their business model designs and generally move in one of the following directions:

~ Toward centralizing business activities such as procurement in order to improve overall operating efficiencies and reduce costs through improved buying power and scale economies
~ Toward reorganizing business activities around customers to improve effectiveness of relationships, enhance overall strategic positioning, and increase revenues

As is often the case with some business activities—first among them, marketing—there is a need to move in both directions simultaneously.

STRUCTURE FOLLOWS STRATEGY

As presented in Chapter 2, your strategy is embodied in your brand architecture, and so that is where you must begin (see Figure 8.2). The brand architecture identifies the individual parts of the brand in order to pinpoint its contribution to customer value creation. The brand architecture is the foundation for the brand positioning, which clearly and concisely articulates how you want your customers to think, feel, and act regarding your brand. It represents the structural integrity of the brand, as well as how that brand is built, how it works, and how the components fit together to deliver meaningful benefits to your customers.

The brand architecture must define and guide everything and everyone associated with the brand. Everyone means *everyone*, not just the marketing people. Marketing is too important to remain only in the marketing department. To fully leverage a compelling brand positioning, all of the brand's activities must focus on the fundamental marketing objective of increasing profitability. If every

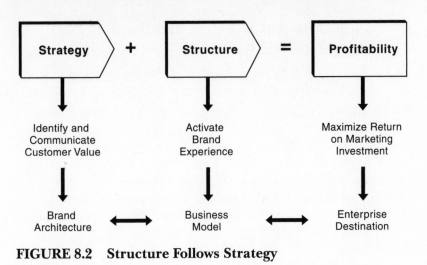

FIGURE 8.2   Structure Follows Strategy

segment of an organization understands the value of brand positioning, then every segment can contribute to a significant growth
in sales and profits. The brand positioning is the strategic compass
by which every program, activity, or initiative that the brand under-
takes, whether directly or indirectly relevant to the consumer, must
be measured.

The concept of brand positioning is so important that it can't be
repeated enough: Any business activity that is inconsistent with the
brand positioning is, at best, a waste of resources. At worst, poor
marketing management can inadvertently destroy the brand you
are attempting to build.

Everything about your business communicates a message: what
you say, what you don't say, what you do, what you don't do. The way
your salesperson dresses can say far more about the performance of
your business than the multi-million-dollar advertising campaign
that you just launched. The condition of your trucks and stores says
more than the beautiful billboard advertising. The attitude of the
customer service representative in the call center sends a stronger
signal than the clever jingle on the radio. Effective marketing
encompasses business design and operations as well as communications. Building a productive, profitable brand experience will
require a total rethink of how you run your business—and that
means keeping an eye on *everything* your business communicates.

USING A BRAND ARCHITECTURE TO ACTIVATE THE BRAND EXPERIENCE

Traditionally, businesses have grown up, evolved, and structured themselves around what they make. Business units, product units, and functional support units are the common structures in place in Global 2000 companies today. Enterprise marketing management demands that the enterprise shift from a *make-centered* to a *sell-centered* business model. In other words, how would you design your business to deliver on your brand promise from the customer's perspective rather than from the company's perspective? Procurement of raw materials, manufacturing, warehousing, shipping—all of these essential activities must keep the customer's best interests at the forefront.

BUSINESS MODEL COMPONENTS

Think of your business model as the collection of assets, capabilities, and activities that you perform to create value for customers (see Figure 8.3). Every enterprise can be defined in terms of the

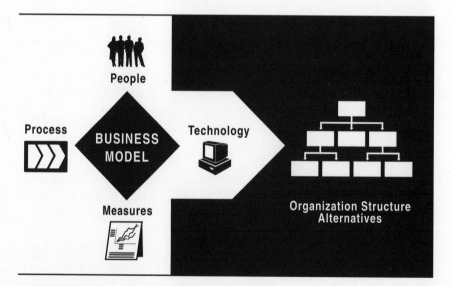

FIGURE 8.3   Business Model Components

business model and the various components that you must build, buy, or borrow in order to deliver on the promise of the brand. These components include the following:

~ **Measures.**   Performance measures must be defined and metrics targets set to monitor your investment in marketing and to hold marketing people and projects accountable for business results. (This concept will be the subject of Chapter 9.) Measures are critical to making decisions on investing the scarce resources of the firm in order to maximize profitability and deliver on the brand promise.

~ **Process.**   Business processes are the recipes for how you get things done across the enterprise. They describe the activities that are required to make, sell, and service your products. Within the marketing function, processes must manage brands, inform product development, interface with sales, run and monitor campaigns, work with outside providers, develop creative executions, and so forth.

~ **Technology.**   In recent years, investment in technology has increased dramatically for most enterprises. The challenge is determining which technologies truly differentiate and drive sustained preference for your brand. Technology innovations in your business model will pay you back if they build on and reinforce an existing strength, advantage, or core competence. Furthermore, you can expect high returns from technology initiatives that reinforce strategic trade-offs and solidify brand positioning, exploit your skills in customer analytics, provide unique access to customer or market data, enable strong service cultures, or accelerate merger and acquisition strategies. But remember: You can save a lot of money by not "keeping up with the Joneses" when it comes to technology innovation—use only the innovations that benefit you, not the ones that everyone else is buying just because they can.

~ **People.**   Everybody in the enterprise must understand their role as a marketer, and marketing must understand every facet of the enterprise. Your business model must have the marketing competency not only to reinforce the brand architecture but also to execute winning marketing strategies and tactics to get you to the destination. Furthermore, your people need to embody the values and beliefs that marketing is about selling, first and foremost, and that they are willing to be held accountable for results. Ensure that you have a culture in place that reinforces the kinds of behavior that are consistent with your brand.

BRAND EXPERIENCE BLUEPRINT (REVISITED)

This concept was first introduced in Chapter 4. The brand experience is simply a way to describe the sum of a customer's interactions with a brand. Of course, a customer's interaction with your brand isn't limited to simply making decisions regarding one product versus another. The brand experience includes the customer's actual experience with the product, as well as every other aspect of interaction with your company. A *brand experience blueprint* allows you to understand every single step in a customer's experience with your brand that reinforces what you stand for and, ideally, activates their purchase intent (see Figure 8.4).

Brand Touch Points (Illustrative)	Identify Need	Evaluate Options	Buy	Use	Obtain Support
Communications					
TV	Emotional (1)	Attribute (2)	N/A	Functional (4)	N/A
Radio	Emotional (2)	Functional (2)	N/A	Functional (4)	N/A
Print	Functional (1)	Emotional (1)	Functional (4)	Emotional (1)	Functional (4)
Outdoor	Functional (2)	Functional (3)	Functional (4)	Functional (3)	N/A
Online/Email	Attribute (1)	Attribute (3)	Functional (4)	Attribute (1)	Attribute (4)
Operations					
Telemarketing	Attribute (2)	Emotional (1)	N/A	Attribute (2)	Attribute (4)
In Store	Functional (3)	Emotional (2)	Functional (4)	Functional (4)	Functional (4)
Direct Sales	Emotional (1)	Functional (1)	Functional (4)	Emotional (1)	N/A
Call Center	Functional (3)	Functional (2)	Functional (4)	Functional (4)	Functional (4)
Direct Marketing	Attribute (3)	Attribute (1)	N/A	N/A	N/A

FIGURE 8.4   Brand Experience Blueprint

STRUCTURAL ALTERNATIVES

There are a wide variety of organizational structures that support the delivery of a productive, profitable brand experience. But before you set off on designing your new organization, it is imperative that you have developed a brand architecture and mapped the type of brand experience that you plan to deliver to your customers through your business model. Jumping right to an organizational restructuring without fully considering your brand and operating strategies will result in a design and structure that is misaligned with the delivery of your brand promise.

Structural alternatives generally are dictated by two key variables (see Figure 8.5):

~ **Degree of centralization**—from highly centralized to highly decentralized
  ○ *Centralized*—activities directed from a corporate center
  ○ *Decentralized*—activities directed by groups within business units that operate independently but ideally within the bounds of the overall brand and business strategy

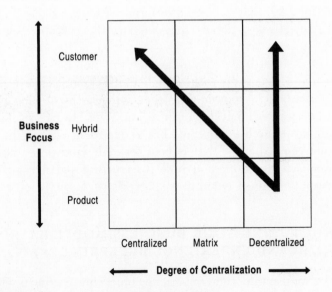

FIGURE 8.5   Structural Alternatives

- ○ *Matrix*—activities directed by groups within business units operate fairly autonomously but report to the corporate center
- ~ *Business focus*—from product-centric to customer-centric
  - ○ *Product-focused*—people structured around specific product or service categories or focused on logical groupings of products and services
  - ○ *Customer-focused*—people structured around relationships with key customers or logical grouping of customers (e.g., demographic or need-based segments)
  - ○ *Hybrid*—people structured around both products and customers (either as separate groups or combined)

Think of these as two structural continuums with many combinations in between.

Furthermore, various business activities within your enterprise may exist in different structural models. For example, many firms have centralized procurement activities and focus their organization into product-centric *categories of spend* in order to leverage scale economies and buying power. The sales organization, on the other hand, may be highly decentralized with sales reps spread across geographies with some even working inside customer organizations. Each business function may require a different structure depending on business objectives and how they support the customer's brand experience.

For most enterprises, the marketing function has evolved into various hybrid structures with some activities centralized in order to consolidate buying power, and other activities highly decentralized to allow for local market optimization. Your strategy, as embodied in the brand architecture and brand experience blueprint, will determine the structure that is best for your enterprise, how to structure each function, and how to structure partnership and alliance relationships beyond your enterprise.

RESTRUCTURING YOUR BUSINESS MODEL BASED ON THE BRAND EXPERIENCE BLUEPRINT

So how do we use the brand experience blueprint to inform critical decisions regarding the way that we create value for customers and then provide the appropriate structure to deliver on the brand promise day in and day out? To help understand this process, let's consider the case of Intouch CellCo, a hypothetical leading provider of wireless communication services.

Intouch CellCo currently faces significant challenges, as the telecommunications industry has undergone significant upheaval over the past 24 months. A lack of differentiation among cellular service providers has led to aggressive switching behavior, or churn, by Intouch CellCo customers. Nearly a quarter of all mobile users have changed service providers within the past year. When questioned, customers cite price as the primary reason for switching and the capabilities of the handset (phone) as the secondary reason. This suggests that the competitive structure of the industry and Intouch CellCo offerings are rapidly losing their distinctiveness. Clearly, Intouch CellCo must reposition its brand and drive to reverse this trend.

THE IMPORTANCE OF SETTING
DESTINATION FOR AN ENTERPRISE

Intouch CellCo set an ambitious goal for itself, intending to become the primary *means of communication* for its customers. It sought to compete not only with other cellular service providers, but with all communications alternatives—wireline, fax, e-mail, pagers, and so forth. Intouch CellCo wants its customers to understand that by using Intouch CellCo products, they will benefit from enriched relationships with people who are close to them, simplify connections in their lives, and receive products and services highly tailored to their specific needs. Only Intouch CellCo can deliver on all of these promises, because it has taken pains to understand its customers and their communities better than anyone else. As a result, Intouch CellCo will make its products and services more attractive to new customers, retain existing customers through new switching costs, and generate more profitable usage of wireless services.

BRAND ARCHITECTURE DICTATES BRAND
EXPERIENCE POSSIBILITIES

To reach its destination, Intouch CellCo needed a breakout strategy to differentiate itself from the other communications alternatives, to create a lasting preference for the Intouch CellCo brand, and to

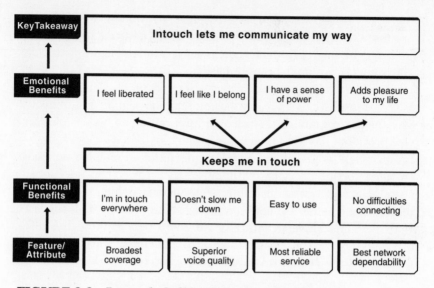

FIGURE 8.6　Intouch CellCo Brand Architecture

determine strategies for increasing the usage of wireless services from its existing customer base. Figure 8.6 shows the Intouch CellCo brand architecture.

After conducting market research to determine the key drivers of purchase intent, Intouch CellCo identified the following benefits that it would have to deliver in order to maintain its relevance in the category, differentiate it from other alternatives, and create true brand preference:

~ Reliable coverage
~ Quickly and easily gets customers connected and keeps them connected
~ Enriches customers' lives by letting them communicate the way they want

BRAND EXPERIENCE BLUEPRINT DRIVES BUSINESS MODEL DESIGN

Of course, Intouch CellCo's ultimate goal is to integrate the brand positioning into customers' every touch point with the brand. To this end, the Intouch CellCo brand experience blueprint (see Figure

	Brand Touch Points	Identify Need	Evaluate Options	Buy	Use	Obtain Service
Communications	TV	Communicate my way	Adds pleasure to my life	N/A	Communicate my way	Adds pleasure to my life
	Print	I belong	Sense of power	Reliable coverage	Superior voice quality	Reliable connection
	Outdoor	In touch everywhere	In touch everywhere	Doesn't slow me down	In touch everywhere	In touch everywhere
Operations	In Store	Communicate my way	Adds pleasure to my life	Doesn't slow me down	Easy to use handsets	Doesn't slow me down
	Call Center	I belong	Sense of power	Doesn't slow me down	N/A	N/A
	Direct Marketing	Communicate my way	Communicate my way	N/A	N/A	Communicate my way

FIGURE 8.7   Intouch CellCo Brand Experience Blueprint

8.7) should provide guidance for execution throughout the Intouch CellCo operations, not just marketing communications. By mapping the brand architecture elements to key customer touch points, Intouch CellCo determined that there were 10 critical functions of the business that directly influence the brand experience (see Figure 8.8).

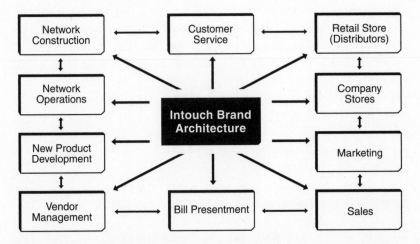

FIGURE 8.8   Integrating Brand Architecture into the Daily Activities of Intouch CellCo

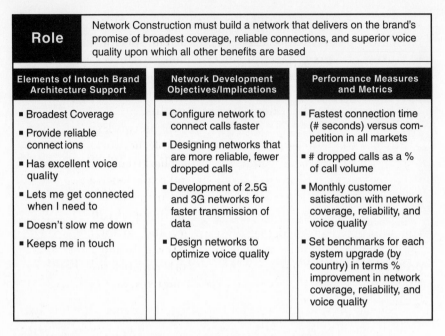

Role	Network Construction must build a network that delivers on the brand's promise of broadest coverage, reliable connections, and superior voice quality upon which all other benefits are based	
Elements of Intouch Brand Architecture Support	**Network Development Objectives/Implications**	**Performance Measures and Metrics**
■ Broadest Coverage ■ Provide reliable connections ■ Has excellent voice quality ■ Lets me get connected when I need to ■ Doesn't slow me down ■ Keeps me in touch	■ Configure network to connect calls faster ■ Designing networks that are more reliable, fewer dropped calls ■ Development of 2.5G and 3G networks for faster transmission of data ■ Design networks to optimize voice quality	■ Fastest connection time (# seconds) versus competition in all markets ■ # dropped calls as a % of call volume ■ Monthly customer satisfaction with network coverage, reliability, and voice quality ■ Set benchmarks for each system upgrade (by country) in terms % improvement in network coverage, reliability, and voice quality

FIGURE 8.9   Drive Out Implications for All Areas of the Business: Network Construction

Each of these functions reinforced emotional benefits, functional benefits, and various product features and attributes of the Intouch CellCo brand. In order to reveal these elements and help each function bring the brand to life at the key customer touch points, Intouch CellCo developed specific business model design briefs for each of the functions. An example of the brief created for the network development team is shown in Figure 8.9 and discussed in the next section. While the network development function of a cellular communications provider would not appear to be connected to the delivery of a brand promise, this group, in fact, plays a critical role in conveying the brand's benefits.

DEVELOPING A BUSINESS MODEL DESIGN BRIEF

The role of the network development group is to build a wireless communications network that delivers on the Intouch CellCo brand promise of best coverage, fast and reliable connections, and excellent voice quality—the foundation upon which all other benefits of the brand architecture are based. The specific brand benefits that this group can influence include attributes like these: "Lets me get connected when I need to," "Doesn't slow me down," and "Keeps me in touch with the most important people"—a powerful mix of emotional and functional benefits.

To ensure delivery of these benefits, the network construction group intends to design faster, more reliable networks that optimize voice quality and drop fewer calls. The group's contribution to the activation of Intouch CellCo brand experience along these dimensions can (and must) be measured in terms of connection times versus competition, percentage of dropped calls, percentage improvement in network coverage, and so forth. In turn, these measures can be used to design rewards and recognition programs that will motivate the network construction group to achieve its objectives, exceed its target metrics, and enhance the brand experience.

By taking this approach, Intouch CellCo effectively shifted the enterprise from a make-centered to a sell-centered business model. The company aligned the business to deliver on its brand promise from the customer's perspective rather than from the company perspective of procuring and distributing handsets, building networks, tracking cell phone usage, and preparing monthly statements. Furthermore, it demonstrated how practically every employee had the potential to impact the customer's brand experience. And, most important, it showed people how their individual actions, when properly focused, could reinforce and enhance the positioning of the brand every day.

CASE STUDY: Aspen Skiing Company

REPOSITIONING ASPEN/SNOWMASS AND ITS COMPETITORS

Aspen/Snowmass is the brand name for four ski/snowboard areas owned by the Aspen Skiing Company. For decades, the town of Aspen has served as a winter playground for the elite, its very name summoning up images of glamour, wealth, and privilege. However, this widely held perception had become a weakness for the resort, as many skiers viewed Aspen/Snowmass to be expensive, hard to get to, and so glitzy as to be unapproachable.

Aspen/Snowmass reigns as one of the premier ski destinations in the world, but it has faced ever-increasing competition from other Colorado and Utah resorts. In the 1990s, the skiing industry declined overall. But when attendance growth for several ski resorts spiked during the 2000–2001 season, Aspen/Snowmass determined that additional marketing and brand architecture help was necessary. The company needed to reposition its brand meaning and inject new life into its operations.

The Aspen/Snowmass loyal visitor profile skewed significantly older than the general skier population, so the resort needed to identify and capture a broader spectrum of skiers (especially younger skiers) to ensure its future prosperity. And the resort had to entice new skiers to try Aspen/Snowmass even though it is not easily reachable. Because of the small size of the airport serving the town of Aspen and the limited population surrounding the resort, most skiers must drive four hours from Denver to get to Aspen, passing more than a dozen quality ski resorts along the way.

The resort did not have the luxury of time for extended planning and program execution. The 2001–2002 season would mark a watershed for the skiing industry, as Utah would be hosting the 2002 Winter Olympic Games. Overall, Utah resorts were expected to see a decline of 10 percent or more in skier days captured due to Olympic events and associated preparation—meaning that an estimated half million skier days would be up for grabs that season. Those Utah resorts would also come out of the 2002 Olympics with worldwide recognition and reputation, thus increasing their appeal for skiers. So Aspen/Snowmass could not afford to stand pat.

Setting the Strategic Brand Destination

Aspen/Snowmass's most valuable visitors are destination skiers— out-of-towners who fly in from locations all over the world for ski vacations, rather than local skiers driving in for day trips or long weekends. The challenge for Aspen was to identify and target those subcategories of destination skiers that represent the greatest opportunity and probability of success for Aspen/Snowmass. The resort's primary competitors were other destination ski resorts in Colorado and Utah. Resorts on the east and west coast tend to draw regional skiers who are less interested in a Rocky Mountain skiing experience. The management team also hypothesized that none of these Rocky Mountain resorts were differentiating themselves significantly. The resorts were marketing generic ski resort features—outstanding powder, rapid lift lines, beautiful weather—rather than the unique features of their own resort. In short, they were selling the category of skiing, not their own particular brand of skiing.

Developing Initial Brand Hypotheses and Validating in the Market

Aspen/Snowmass's initial brand positioning hypothesis held that there was a substantial segment of the skiing population that would be less concerned about price and more concerned about the total vacation experience. While the resort will never be the least expensive skiing destination in the region because of its cost structure, the management team believed that there is a sizable group of skiers that would be willing to pay for a superior experience. In addition to hosting world-class skiing, the town of Aspen/Snowmass is a rustic former mining community that features first-rate dining, shopping, and lodging. No other resort can deliver Aspen/Snowmass's combination of outstanding skiing and top-shelf nightlife.

To test and validate its preliminary assessments and strategic hypotheses, interviews were conducted with 800 active destination skiers, defined as skiers living outside of Colorado and Utah who have skied at least twice in the past three years and at least once in Colorado or Utah during that time. The surveys focused on segmenting the U.S. destination skier population according to their skiing attitudes, behaviors, and demographics, while also identifying the key purchase drivers for Colorado/Utah destination ski resorts.

The testing indicated that three key segments of interest accounted for only 48 percent of the skiing population, but represented 90 percent of the total potential Aspen/Snowmass ski days. These desirable skier segments shared a core set of attitudes about what they were looking for in a ski vacation that cut across demographic profiles and skiing ability.

Bringing the Brand to Life at Every Customer Touch Point

With the knowledge of the most viable skier segments in hand, the management team developed a brand architecture and positioning promoting the features and benefits unique to Aspen/Snowmass that were most likely to motivate the target population to visit the resort. These segments were already sold on the benefits of skiing, but they needed to be sold on the benefits of skiing at Aspen/Snowmass in particular. The brand positioning they developed tapped into the key customer benefit that the target segments craved in a ski vacation and allowed Aspen/Snowmass to differentiate itself so that it did not have to compete on price, as many of its competitors were doing.

The management team also repositioned what had been seen as one of Aspen/Snowmass's greatest drawbacks—its location—into a competitive advantage. Aspen/Snowmass's most desirable segments could be persuaded that while the resort is harder to reach, the extra effort was worth it to get away from more crowded roadside highway resorts. The Aspen/Snowmass location hurdle was thus repositioned as a unique benefit, since it protects the total vacation experience from the burdensome local traffic that clogs the resorts located closer to Denver.

Most important, the Aspen/Snowmass management team recognized that the new brand positioning must be brought to life across all customer touch points (see Figure 8.10)—creating a highly differentiated brand experience, not just another advertising campaign. The new Aspen/Snowmass tag line—"the difference is night and day"—builds the initial expectation of the total Aspen ski vacation experience, highlighting both the on- and off-slope virtues of the resort. The brand positioning is reinforced through the reservations and customer service operators, and is further delivered by the actions of the ski school, hotel staff, restaurants, and mountain operations. Business design briefs were created for each of the critical stakeholder groups that would have an opportunity to impact and reinforce the Aspen/Snowmass brand experience (including mountain restaurant operations, ski and snowboard schools, pro mountain sports, mountain operations, lodging and reservations, central ticket sales, and human resources). To be successful, all of these groups must work together to bring the new brand positioning to life.

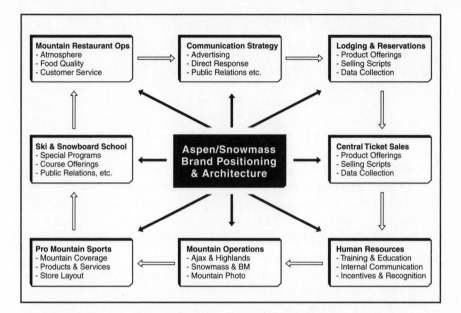

FIGURE 8.10   The difference is "night and day" at every customer touch point

The Results

The short-term results have been remarkable for Aspen/Snowmass. At the outset of the 2001–2002 ski season, Aspen/Snowmass was rated the number one resort in the United States by *Skiing* magazine. This was the resort's first top rating ever, up from number four the previous year. In addition, despite a 30 to 40 percent downturn for the skiing industry in Colorado during the first few months of the 2001–2002 season (due to the impact of the September 11 terrorist attacks and the global recession), Aspen/Snowmass saw a downturn of only 10 to 15 percent. In fact, during the critical 2001 holiday skiing period, Aspen/Snowmass skier visits actually exceeded the previous year's levels. What's more, Aspen/Snowmass achieved this without resorting to the type of deep price discounts made by its competitors.

At the close of the traditional 2001–2002 ski season, Aspen/ Snowmass's earnings saw an increase of 36 percent from the previous year. And the resort's skier days dropped only 4 percent from the prior year, while key competitor Vail saw its skier days drop more significantly versus the previous year.

MARKETER'S SCIENTIFIC METHOD: RESTRUCTURING BASED ON BRAND EXPERIENCE

Following are the steps to take in restructuring your marketing based on brand experience.

Step 1: Ensure That Everyone Understands the Destination

If people in your enterprise don't know where the brand is headed and *exactly* how you want your customers to think, feel, and act with regard to your brand, there is no way that you'll be able to achieve your business objectives. Take the time to make sure that everyone involved with your operation—your people, your critical suppliers, partners, service providers, and anyone who represents your brand to customers—understands your ultimate destination. Crystallize your destination in a *destination statement* (see "Marketer's Scientific Method" in Chapter 2 for more detail) that everyone can reference and use to validate marketing and operational changes that could impact your brand. Consider enterprise-specific questions such as, "If we run this advertisement will it help us get to our destination?" and "If we make this change to our script in the call center, will it help us get to our destination?"

Step 2: Create the Brand Experience Blueprint

Generally speaking, customers contact your business to identify their needs, evaluate their options, buy products or services, use those products and services, and possibly obtain support. At every one of these stages, they experience your brand. The goal is to map the key benefits from your brand architecture—the aspects that you know motivate purchase intent—to each of the stages of the brand experience. Your enterprise and associated partners can create brand preference by bringing the benefits to life as you inform, propose, sell, educate, and provide support to your customers. Obviously, these broad stages will have to be broken down into specific interaction points unique to your business (telemarketing, direct sales interactions, financial transactions, call center interactions, field service interactions, and so on). As part of this step, you should also identify key stakeholders inside and outside the enterprise that have accountability. The brand spans the entire enterprise, so stakeholders may end up representing many of the functional departments across your business, including finance, operations, sales, procurement, and legal.

Step 3: Develop Business Model Design Briefs and Enlist Key Stakeholders

Now that you have developed the brand experience blueprint, the key stakeholders across your extended enterprise accountable for customer interactions, and the specific brand benefits that can be activated at each touch point, you are ready to begin designing the optimal business model to deliver a productive, profitable brand experience. Create cross-functional teams to design the business model from the customer's perspective—use the brand experience blueprint as your guide. For every key customer interaction, a business model design brief would specify requirements for performing the following tasks:

~ Characterizing the interaction in customer terms (e.g., requesting information about handsets, coverage area, and usage rates)

~ Identifying and prioritizing the elements of the brand to activate (e.g., "Keeps you in touch with people who matter to you," "Lets you get connected when you need to," "Best coverage of all providers")

~ Identifying a key stakeholder accountable for the brand experience (e.g., inbound sales)

~ Setting out the roles and responsibilities of the stakeholder (e.g., inform, propose, and sell)

~ Determining the people skills and capabilities required to deliver the optimal brand experience (product knowledge, solution selling, sensitivity training, and so forth)

~ Establishing the changes to current business processes required (e.g., restructuring the sales script to focus on emotional benefits first, functional benefits, and finally features)

~ Setting out the customer data and insights required in order to activate the brand experience (e.g., current provider, segment profile, usage profile)

~ Noting modifications required to existing technologies
  or requirements for new enabling technologies (e.g.,
  integrating the customer insights database with the call
  center contact management system)
~ Establishing performance measures and metrics to evaluate activation of the brand experience and associated
  business outcomes (e.g., close rate, incremental usage
  rate, brand affiliation with best coverage ratings)

It is critical to engage the key stakeholders in the business
model design efforts—people will support what they help to create!
Try to include external stakeholders as well, especially people who
are part of your extended enterprise and come into frequent contact with your customers. These individuals have significant influence over the brand experience but may feel like they have not had
a say in how you position your products and services in the market.

Step 4: Develop an Organization Structure to Support the Business Model

At this point, you are ready to develop the organization structure—
the hierarchy of jobs, reporting structures, spans, and layers required
to support the activation and sustained delivery of the brand experience. Again, it is critical to engage all key stakeholders from the previous steps in this exercise to ensure alignment and commitment to
the new structure. Depending on the diversity of needs of the customer segments that are served, you may end up with an organization structure that is highly centralized at one extreme, highly
decentralized at the other extreme, or some form of hybrid or matrix
structure in the middle. Based on the roles and responsibilities
defined in the previous step, you can begin to logically group activities together and define jobs. As a general rule, customer touch
points should be logically grouped together to minimize the number
of handoffs between various stakeholder groups. Based on these
groupings and the relative size of the customer segments, you can
begin to determine the level of centralization or decentralization as
well as the spans and layers that will be required to deliver the brand
experience.

9

MEASURE INVESTMENT
PERFORMANCE

Despite the need to rethink their business model, when faced
with economic uncertainties and increased pressures to
achieve quarterly targets, most corporate leaders respond by
battening down the hatches, focusing on the necessities, and riding
out the storm. The year following September 11, 2001, saw massive
layoffs, deferment of investment decisions, reactive decision making, more inward focus (and, consequently, less focus on customers),
and deep cuts in discretionary expenses. These discretionary cuts
also include disturbingly large slices into spending on marketing initiatives. Many shortsighted corporate leaders continue to insist that
they cannot afford—or, worse, do not need—marketing in a slow
economy. Effective marketing drives customers to businesses more
frequently and persuades them to buy more products and services
for more money—no matter what the economic situation.

MARKETING IS AN INVESTMENT—AND
NEEDS TO BE MEASURED AS SUCH

Companies like Coca-Cola, Starbucks, and Ritz-Carlton have
become leaders in their industries because they have embraced

the fact that marketing is an *investment,* not an expense. Further, they rigorously analyze their investment alternatives and adopt proven investment management practices, such as ROI analysis, to evaluate *any* marketing initiative or campaign. Given the fact that marketing initiatives, by their very nature, can be difficult to measure, Zyman Marketing Group has developed proprietary techniques for facilitating the return on marketing investment (ROMI) analysis process and determining which marketing activities actually create value for the enterprise and at what cost. Zyman Marketing Group refers to this methodology as *activity-based marketing* (see "Marketer's Scientific Method" later in this chapter).

Businesses that do not apply these rigorous financial management approaches to marketing projects have experienced a precipitous falloff in their valuation over time. The reason is simple: Without an awareness of ROMI and a comprehensive set of marketing investment management tactics, leaders continue to make the wrong decisions and inexorably erode their company's value. If you're running a business and you think that marketing is something that you just don't get, you're probably spending money in the wrong places. It's time to reevaluate your priorities.

STOP BUDGETING FOR MARKETING AND START INVESTING WISELY

In many instances, business leaders consider a collection of marketing initiatives as a bundle of expenses, simply another entry in an annual marketing budget. Visionary business leaders don't budget for marketing; they develop a marketing investment strategy. Businesses that still attempt to figure out how much they will spend on marketing by extrapolating how much they believe they will sell— for example, "Let's go with a 10 percent marketing budget"—are not really marketing, they're just marking time. In general, marketing managers receive minimal training in return on marketing investment measures, and many highly skilled marketers still do not use this measurement tool accurately or strategically. In its simplest form, ROMI can be calculated as follows:

$$ROMI = \frac{(DCF - MI)}{MI}$$

where:

> DCF = discounted cash flow. The future flow of gains and losses over time must be discounted back to the present (net present value) to reflect the time value of money.
> MI = marketing investments required to generate the cash flow.

A key objective of the marketing organization should be to maximize ROMI for the firm—as Sergio Zyman would say, "To sell more stuff to more people more often for more money in the most efficient manner." The ROMI measure can be broken down into subcomponents to make it more actionable for the marketer (see Figure 9.1).

For instance, to maximize ROMI in the preceding calculation, it is imperative to increase DCF while decreasing MI. Intuitively, this makes sense: Increase the cash flow and decrease the investment required to generate the cash flow, and you've maximized

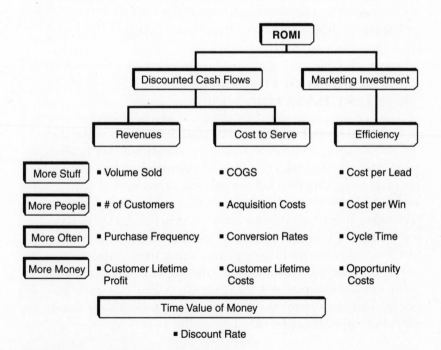

FIGURE 9.1   What Drives ROMI?

your return. So, what makes up DCF? Many factors influence this value, but, stated simply, they are:

More sales.   If you increase the volume of goods and services that you sell, you should have a positive impact on DCF—assuming, of course, that you are not selling them for less than what it costs you to produce them (COGS = cost of goods sold).

More people.   By increasing your total number of customers, you should also have a positive impact on DCF. Again, this assumes that the lifetime value of the customer exceeds your cost to acquire the customer (acquisition costs).

More often.   By increasing customer frequency of purchase or usage, you're really selling more stuff to more people. Of course, the same caveats apply here regarding maintaining margins on every incremental sale. A key measure that drives DCF is conversion rate. If you have low rates of conversion (customers buy less of your stuff less often) you will negatively impact DCF.

More money.   Through your marketing efforts, you may be able to command a premium price for your products and services. Pricing strategy and how well you maintain prices and avoid discounting will have a significant impact on DCF. Customer lifetime profit is a key measure for understanding how DCF will be impacted over the long-term based on the amount of profit generated by each customer. Obviously, lowering total cost to serve the customer over time (customer lifetime cost) will also have a significant impact on DCF.

Most efficiently.   Measuring and optimizing what you invest in marketing is critical. In general, you should continue to invest in marketing until you begin to see diminishing returns on your investment. Other critical ratios to track to determine the efficiency of your marketing investment include:

~ *Cost per lead:*   On average, what does it cost to generate each lead?

~ *Cost per win:*   On average, what does it cost to win each deal with each customer?

~ *Deal cycle time:*   How long does it take to close a deal from start to finish?

~ *Opportunity cost:*   What other ways could the marketing investment dollars have been used to drive higher returns and increase profitability for the enterprise?

Marketing assets are just as important on a balance sheet as any traditional assets, such as manufacturing plants and production equipment. Business leaders should approach marketing assets in the same way, by aggressively tracking return on marketing assets (ROMA). Getting started is a simple process. Consider the new rules of marketing investment, as outlined in Table 9.1. If your business thinking falls on the left side of the table, you need to move right. To do so, you need to look at how to apply financial theory to the marketing function. You must use measures and metrics that will help ensure that you maximize the efficiency and effectiveness of your marketing investment, regardless of the external economic condition. You also need to consider how to shift the values and beliefs of your people to achieve the greatest returns on marketing investments and hold everyone in the enterprise accountable for results.

In marketing, as in life, the conventional wisdom is not always wise. Even in recessionary times, companies can ill afford to ignore their customers and marketing outreach efforts in order to save a few bucks. Purchasing still takes place; customers still attach themselves to new companies and new products. Indeed, the depressed

Table 9.1   The New Rules of Marketing Investment

From	*To*
Marketing is an expense.	Marketing is an investment.
Allocate marketing budgets.	Create strategic marketing investment plans.
Give budgets to people.	Give budgets to projects.
Measure budget variances.	Measure ROMI and ROMA.
Expand marketing asset base.	Maximize existing marketing assets.
Collect lots of data.	Collect lots of relevant data and derive insights.

economy offers the truly innovative companies a distinct advantage. Just imagine how much further ahead you'll be if you're running while everyone else is standing still.

MAKE ROMI A RELIGION, NOT JUST A FAD

While the marketing department is responsible for specific marketing programs, the programs are much more effective when all departments act in sync, as Chapter 3 demonstrated. For example, if your brand stands for the highest-quality products in your category, you target consumers who are interested in high quality and don't mind paying a high price for it. Your marketing department leverages the elements of the marketing mix to target those consumers, driving sales for your product. To a certain degree, setting a high price point connotes both high value and high quality. Your sales force must be trained and provided incentives to minimize any discounting that would tarnish the brand.

Further, the product must be manufactured to the highest quality standards in order to reinforce the brand experience managed by marketing. In the unfortunate event that defects do occur, your distributors and field service organizations must stand ready to act immediately to address any quality breakdowns. As a result, the brand positioning is completely in sync and reinforced by the execution of the pricing strategy, sales incentive programs, manufacturing process, channel strategy, and service commitment. The elements of the marketing mix and all customer touch points are harmonized to deliver on those critical emotional and functional benefits that build a lifelong brand experience—of course, all with the intent of maximizing sales and profits.

Now consider the case in which, again, to drive purchase intent, the brand delivers a functional benefit of high quality and targets consumers who are not price sensitive. However, in this instance, the price is set too low. At the very least, the low price will undercut your company's potential profit, and it will also potentially repel those very customers you wish to attract. While the interplay of price, quality, and brand is driven largely by category dynamics, there are many examples in which customers use price to connote value. And if the brand stands for high quality but is actually manufactured to a lesser standard in order to maintain margins, customers will be disappointed. While the marketing programs you execute may appear to achieve their intended purpose, because of the pricing and manufacturing decisions, then any marketing programs executed under these conditions will generate suboptimal results.

It's the same when aiming for the profitability of the firm: A company is much more effective when all functions act in sync. All departments, all employees, should want the firm to be profitable. Without profitability, no one will have a job in the long term. Therefore all employees have a vested interest and responsibility in contributing to the profitability of the firm, and all need to work in sync to achieve this profitability.

Just as marketing programs are more effective when everyone supports the same strategy and objectives, so is profitability. Using ROMI analysis enables the firm to ensure that the money invested in the marketing activities of the business generates a sufficient return. ROMI ensures that the entire firm is consistently measuring its marketing investments.

The firm invests funds in many ways in order to make a profit. It invests in the manufacture of the product, making trade-offs in manufacture that result in either a high-quality or a high-value product. It invests in its distribution, often trading cost for time. It invests in marketing, in order to build demand for a product and sell more. It invests in customer service in order to build repeat sales.

The firm also invests in marketing campaigns. These campaigns are necessary to generate primary demand and enhance sales. And while the campaigns may be evaluated to some degree by increased sales, that factor tends to be only a side note, often lost in the glitz, glamour, and hype. If a campaign doesn't result in increased sales, it is easy to blame pricing, manufacturing, or even something as uncontrollable as the weather.

Every marketing campaign needs to be measured on its bottom-line impact to the firm. Not on awareness, not on market share; customer awareness and market share are not indicators of profitability. All marketing initiatives need to be measured on ROMI to show that they are worth the investment and to help evaluate where additional marketing funds can be effectively invested to increase sales and profits.

WHAT NEEDS TO CHANGE?

First, every program in marketing needs to be measured against the same scale: How does this program impact sales and profits? Granted, there are many reasons that this is difficult to do, and you can predict the responses: "No customer responds directly to a program and runs out and buys our product"; "Linking our marketing programs to sales figures is too difficult to do." But difficult doesn't mean impossible, and if you can figure out how to do it, think how far ahead of your competitors you'll be.

At its heart, the concept is simple: Each campaign or marketing initiative must have one person who is held accountable for its contribution to profits (and losses). In other words, every initiative gets evaluated like a P&L statement, on the following criteria:

~ **Every campaign or marketing initiative.** You measure the results of each and every program, no exceptions. If you aren't measuring the results, then why are you even running the campaign?

~ **One person who is held accountable.** You can't hold a group accountable for a result—pinning responsibility on multiple individuals just doesn't work. There needs to be *one* person who is held accountable for the amount invested in each initiative and for ensuring that the program achieves its targeted sales objectives. And because this person is accountable for specific, measurable results, then specific, measurable results will be important to everyone who reports to this person as well.

~ **Its contribution to profits (and losses).** Each marketing initiative needs to have a P&L. This includes sales goals, as well as detailed information on investments made in conducting various activities as part of the initiative.

In order to hold one person accountable for the ROMI of a program, that person needs specific financial information about that program on a timely basis, like how much the program is costing. So you need to track the funds invested in that initiative. Any time money is spent to support the initiative, it needs to be accounted for. It needs to be clear exactly how much you are investing in the initiative. It also needs to be clear how those funds are invested. Is it invested in production of advertising? In media buys? In promotional events? In creative fees? This information will provide valuable insights into the best ways to invest your funds, especially once you measure the results.

You also need to track the results of the investment. This means that you track the impact of the initiative on corporate sales in hard dollars, not ephemeral measurements like brand awareness. This activity has implications for both the structural and the cultural aspects of managing any marketing program.

Consider the structural elements first. The structural elements provide the support needed to measure the impact of your marketing programs. Two key structural elements need to be in place:

~ An accounting system that tracks marketing initiatives in terms of P&L
~ A performance management system between marketing and sales

The accounting system must enable costs to be tracked for each program, at a level of detail where you can analyze the impact of various investments on the program. For example, were programs equally effective regardless of the amount spent on marketing? The system also needs to communicate sales results for each program. And this data must be delivered on a timely basis.

Marketing and sales need to be more tightly integrated. For example, say marketing creates a program involving a promotion in Peoria. Then the marketing person who runs that program needs the sales results for Peoria. He or she needs to understand all the elements that went into the sales and how the program could have improved sales. If possible, he or she can make changes to the program to drive an increase in sales, and then track whether they were successful.

MAKING THE MEASURES MEANINGFUL ON A DAY-TO-DAY BASIS

So you change your accounting system and relationship with sales. These alterations are fruitless unless you actually look at the measures and utilize the relationship with sales. How, then, do you change the culture of an entire group?

Begin with the premise that employees will set their priorities to align with the priorities of their boss. Therefore, start by selecting key people to be accountable for each program. These people must be influential senior leaders, and they need influence both above and below them in the hierarchy.

Once you select these individuals, their incentives must be aligned with managing the P&L for their programs. They must also effectively communicate the progress of their program to their senior management and those outside marketing. Everyone who works with these leaders must expect to hear about the P&L of their programs.

As always, these leaders will rely on their teams to help them build a successful program. If it is a priority to this leader, it will be a priority to all who report to him or her—including outside service providers that may not be direct reports but that influence and potentially impact ROMI for specific initiatives. They need to share the financial information with their teams in terms of specific performance metrics that are actionable and clearly linked to desired business objectives.

For example, consider again the Intouch CellCo case introduced in Chapter 8. Advertising is one of the most effective ways to communicate the most complex emotional benefits of the Intouch CellCo wireless communications brand. So, using the Intouch CellCo brand architecture to inform the creative process, the company determined that the primary objective of the advertising must be to create the belief among customers that Intouch CellCo can deliver key emotional benefits by depicting customers receiving these benefits in situations and occasions that are relevant to various customer groups. A secondary objective is to indirectly show how Intouch CellCo adds a little pleasure to customers' lives by delivering key functional benefits. Of course, the desired business outcomes from the advertising campaign are to increase customer retention rate, attract new customers, and increase overall usage of the service by new and existing customers. The Intouch CellCo executive accountable for this campaign needs to communicate with his or her team in terms of specific, actionable measures that link directly to these desired objectives and outcomes. The measures listed in Table 9.2 were created and monitored throughout the campaign.

It's important to note that these measures must be consistent in both their application and their delivery. Team members must

Table 9.2   Intouch CellCo Performance Management

Performance Indicators	Business Outcome Measures (and Metrics)
Increase in preference for Intouch CellCo brand	Customer retention rate (+15%)
Spot recall, message recall, and linkage to Intouch CellCo brand	Total number of new customers (+500,000 accounts)
Share of voice and share of market (advertising effectiveness)	Average minutes of usage per customer (+250 minutes)

always have access to the appropriate information, while upper management must be able to compare results from different marketing campaigns on a relevant qualitative and quantitative basis. If you know what works and why in one effort, you can easily translate that success to another effort—as long as the data remains consistent across campaigns. Keeping every branch of the company, from front-line sales to upper management, abreast of campaign activities gives everyone a greater stake in and understanding of all campaign efforts.

COMMUNICATE THE EFFECTIVENESS OF MARKETING PROGRAMS

To communicate in a foreign country, it helps to speak the language rather than rely on native speakers to translate or understand yours. Speaking the language makes it easier to request help from others, to do what you need to do, and to get what you want.

To communicate with your customers, it helps to speak their language. You use current slang and styles to reach the teenage market; you use more mainstream language and conservative styles to market a product to senior citizens. Speaking their language increases the probability that you will get what you want: increased sales.

To communicate with others in your company, it helps to speak their language. While some nonmarketers might understand marketing lingo, you are hoping they can translate "marketing-ese" the way you want them to. Avoid this problem—speak their language to minimize any errors in translation.

Speaking their language not only minimizes confusion, but also enables you to show that marketing is working toward the same goals. So if the rest of the company measures success on ROMI, then marketing needs to speak of their work in terms of ROMI. This doesn't mean just when you are giving a report or just at the senior level. This means *all the time, every day.* "What did you do to increase sales and profits today?" needs to be a key, constant question.

Just as the company knows how many products will be manufactured and at what cost, the company should also know what marketing programs are in place. The ROMI of programs, and the driving factors, must be discussed in executive meetings, in staff meetings with the marketing folks, anytime marketing discusses performance, and anytime anyone outside of marketing discusses performance. Measuring the ROMI of your marketing programs will provide valuable information on how to spend your marketing funds.

LEARNING AND IMPROVING BASED ON RESULTS

Just possessing knowledge isn't enough. For instance, every automobile manufacturer knows how an internal combustion engine works and why four wheels are the optimal number for a passenger vehicle. What will separate you from your competitors is the use of that information, over and over again. By obtaining timely feedback on your campaigns, linking your ROMI to sales programs and data, and keeping a constant watch on where exactly your dollars are going and whether they are succeeding, you can course-correct as often as necessary in order to take your company to the top.

At Intouch CellCo, a lack of differentiation among wireless service providers was leading to increased customer switching behavior, or *churn.* Intouch CellCo executives had always believed that the primary reason for switching was driven by improvements in network performance and extended coverage. As competitors upgraded their systems, customers would switch to get better service. Interestingly enough, after analyzing the reasons for switching among contract and prepaid customers, satisfaction with service or coverage did not even make the top 10 reasons cited for switching. Price was the number one reason, and the handset (type of phone) was second. The customer focus on price demonstrated the fact that there was little differentiation among competitors, and customers were just seeking the best deal—no brand really held any relevance, and price had become the only discriminating feature. With this insight in mind, Intouch CellCo executives could course-correct, shift marketing investments away from a "better sameness" positioning in the category, and attempt to build real brand differentiation and preference.

MAKING TRADE-OFFS

In a perfect world, you'd have endless cash flow to spiral out into campaign after campaign, running all kinds of ideas up the flagpole. The truth, of course, is that trade-offs need to be made; resources are not infinite, and you need to know where and how to invest your marketing dollars to get the best return. ROMI allows you to make trade-offs by giving you reliable data on exactly how much you've invested in each campaign. Knowing where and how your funds are invested allows you to track and compare how each investment is performing. With this information in hand, you can determine where the next round of cash should be invested, and— just as important—where it should not. Rather than spraying money around indiscriminately—or even equally—you can target the regions, customers, or markets where your investment is taking hold (more details on this in Chapter 10).

DIFFERENCES TO EXPECT IN RESULTS AND IN CULTURE

If it's possible to generate any truisms in marketing, here's one: Doing the same thing over and over again will yield—at best—the same results. If you're not headed toward where you want to be, your present course isn't going to take you there. So you can use ROMI as a compass to help determine your direction and properly reallocate your resources. You (and your company) can learn from what works and what doesn't, and can measure success in hard dollars. With such statistics in hand, marketing no longer needs to rely on ethereal measurements such as "awareness" or "desirability." Now, you can communicate more clearly the results of marketing campaigns, which will in turn generate support for winning efforts throughout the organization. In the end, this leads to decisions based on sound strategy and statistics, not hunches or tradition— and by any measure, that's a positive change.

CASE STUDY: Harrah's Casinos

MARKETING INVESTMENT STRATEGY YIELDS A PRODUCTIVE, PROFITABLE BRAND EXPERIENCE

There is no industry more dedicated to the power of marketing investment management than casino gaming. Gamblers are creatures of habit, and no gaming corporation has done a better job of tracking, analyzing, and capitalizing on those habits than Harrah's. At its 25 casinos around the country, Harrah's learns everything possible about its customers, and then presents specifically targeted offers to them based on their value to the corporation, their responsiveness, and their willingness to spend.

At a central processing office in Memphis, Harrah's compiles an incredibly detailed record of every movement and every bet of every valued customer in all of its casinos. Harrah's can monitor the number of machines the customer plays, the number of wagers made, the average size of bets, and the total money deposited in machines (called the *coin-in*). Before a customer has even arrived home from a visit to a casino, Harrah's has compiled enough information on them to build a detailed profile of their gaming habits, a plan for enticing them back to the casino, and even an individual profit-and-loss projection that will aid in future marketing investment in the customer.

Harrah's tracks customer information by using a plastic loyalty card that valued customers slide into slot machines and card tables while they play. The benefit for the company is obvious; the information gathered on the customer is invaluable and is used to refine its database, now segmented into 90 behavior-driven demographic targets. Each segment receives its own custom-tailored direct-mail incentives.

For their part, customers can earn platinum or diamond status based on their gambling levels. They can visit www.harrahs.com to find their point levels and learn more about benefits. Based on which customers choose which benefit packages, Harrah's can continue to refine and improve its marketing investment.

Conventional wisdom would hold that the slots players, playing only a quarter or a dollar at a time, are Harrah's least valuable customers. And conventional wisdom would be dead wrong. Slots and other electronic gaming machines account for the majority of Harrah's $3.7 billion in annual revenue and constitute more than 80 percent of the company's operating profit. Because it has tracked and retained its slots players, Harrah's has grown to be the second-largest gaming company in the United States, behind only MGM Entertainment. Harrah's also boasts the highest three-year investment return in the industry. In just the first two years of its Total Rewards program, Harrah's saw a $100 million increase in revenue from customers who gambled at more than one Harrah's casino.

So how does Harrah's track its 25 million customers? With a combination of technology and strategic analysis. The company begins with four key pieces of information—gender, age, area of residence, and games played—and uses that information to offer early predictions of which customers will become the biggest spenders. The company designs appropriate marketing strategies to lure customers back. The goal is not a product-based one—say, designing games to reach particular revenue levels—but rather a customer-based one, working to maximize revenue from individual customers, regardless of which games they play.

Each of the demographic factors demands its own series of incentives. Out-of-town customers typically receive discounts on hotel rooms or transportation, while local customers receive cash, food, and entertainment incentives. Early expiration dates encourage customers to return quickly or switch from competitors. Harrah's tracks each incentive based on response rates and return on investment, and adjusts future incentives accordingly.

Analysis of customer data found that the 30 percent of Harrah's customers who spent between $100 and $500 per visit accounted for 80 percent of company revenues and almost 100 percent of profits. Those gamblers were typically local residents, who visited their nearby Harrah's frequently.

With this data in hand, Harrah's marketing teams developed a profile of the ideal Harrah's customer. As it turns out, the ideal gambler is a 62-year-old woman who lives within 30 minutes of a casino and plays dollar video poker. These ladies typically have substantial disposable cash, plenty of time on their hands, and easy access to a Harrah's regional casino.

Harrah's has made an intensive, extensive marketing investment, and it's now beginning to pay off. The lesson for other companies is clear—learn who your best customers are, or you're liable to lose them.

MARKETER'S SCIENTIFIC METHOD: ACTIVITY-BASED MARKETING (ABM)

By applying activity-based costing theory to marketing, you can establish a rigorous process for evaluating which marketing activities create value. In turn, you can use this information to develop a robust, fact-based decision-making process for how marketing investments are made. The overall objective of this activity-based marketing (ABM) analysis is to maximize the return on marketing investment (ROMI) that an enterprise can achieve. ABM includes tools for measuring and analyzing ROMI, and it represents a structured methodology to perform the following:

- ~ Apply scientific discipline to maximize the return on every marketing dollar spent across the enterprise
- ~ Optimize the performance of each marketing channel and the portfolio of channels overall (i.e., which channels perform better than others? Where should we invest labor and dollars?)
- ~ Model what-if investment scenarios
- ~ Forecast the number of leads needed per month, per channel to achieve revenue objectives
- ~ Provide a common language and fact base for the marketing and executive teams to make informed decisions

When appropriately implemented, ABM delivers substantial benefits to an enterprise:

- ~ Laying out a road map to success for each business unit across an enterprise, based upon the expected effectiveness and efficiency of each marketing activity, initiative and/or campaign, and so on
- ~ Identifying risks and critical success factors to hit performance targets

~ Providing visibility into the number of leads required at each stage of the sales process in order to achieve financial objectives—giving the management team sufficient time to take corrective action

~ Aligning enterprise marketing and customer strategies with operational investments (i.e., people, process, and technology)

The power of ABM comes from the insights your management team gains as a result of conducting the analysis, asking the right questions, and gaining a new understanding of your business. ROMI tools *alone* do not provide the answers; rather, they provide data on performance and a framework for asking pointed questions. Of course, as discussed in this chapter, organizational involvement and buy-in of the analysis is critical.

Your goal should be to conduct the ABM analysis with the appropriate level of rigor to provide "good enough" data for understanding performance, identifying opportunities, and modeling the future. Above all, avoid analysis paralysis—don't spend so much time looking at your plans that you don't have time to implement them.

Step 1: Understand Past Performance

The first step requires an intimate understanding of where you are in your business and where you have been. This begins with identifying all marketing activities that you perform to reach your target customers. It is important to break down your activities in sufficient detail to ensure that you can reveal and measure the things that really help generate value for customers and for your business. For example, if you think one of your key activities is driving brand preference, you may want to consider breaking this down into several more detailed activities that you believe help drive preference for your brand. You may publish a newsletter, maintain a web site, or conduct seminars, each of which drives preference for your brand. So instead of having an activity called "drive brand preference," you may have several activities in which you invest, such as "publish newsletter" or "maintain web site." Give marketing activities clear names and develop consistent descriptions; otherwise, it will be difficult to track revenues and costs associated with each activity and the value of the analysis will be compromised.

Table 9.3   Sample Scorecard

ID	Activity	Revenue	Avg. Deal Size	Activity % of Revenue	# of Leads
1	Activity 1	$ 100,000	$ 100,000	2%	6
2	Activity 2	$ 150,000	$ 75,000	3%	4
3	Activity 3	$ 600,000	$ 300,000	10%	6
4	Activity 4	$ 500,000	$ 250,000	8%	3
5	Activity 5	$ 500,000	$ 250,000	8%	10
6	Activity 6	$ 3,400,000	$ 309,000	57%	25
7	Activity 7	$ 600,000	$ 150,000	10%	20
8	Activity 8	$ —	$ —	0%	30
9	Activity 9	$ 100,000	$ 50,000	2%	16
10	Activity 10	$ —	$ —	0%	—
11	Activity 11	$ —	$ —	0%	—
12	Activity 12	$ —	$ —	0%	—
13	Activity 13	$ —	$ —	0%	—
14	Activity 14	$ —	$ —	0%	—
15	Activity 15	$ —	$ —	0%	—
16	Activity 16	$ —	$ —	0%	—
	TOTAL	$ 5,950,000		100%	120

Next, try to attribute customer revenue to each activity. This will allow you to compute average, maximum, minimum, and standard deviation of deal sizes by activity and begin to identify opportunities. To start with, keep it simple. Try to tie the source of customer leads to specific activities. At this stage you should also allocate marketing labor costs and discretionary costs to each activity. Once this has been completed, you should begin to get a clearer understanding of which marketing activities actually generate the highest return and drive your business. Table 9.3 shows a sample scorecard that results from Step 1.

Step 2: Model the Future and Perform What-If Analysis

The next step is to model the future performance of your business and determine how to optimize investments. There are two different approaches. *Top-down analysis* is used to determine how to opti-

Table 9.3   *(Continued)*

# of Wins	% of Deals	Total Activity Cost	Cost Per Lead (4)	Cost per Win	Activity COS/Rev
1	4%	$ 22,500	$ 3,750	$ 22,500	23%
2	7%	$ 19,000	$ 4,750	$ 9,500	13%
2	7%	$ —	$ —	$ no cost	0%
2	7%	$ 4,000	$ 1,333	$ 2,000	1%
2	7%	$ 3,000	$ 300	$ 1,500	1%
11	7%	$ 50,613	$ 2,025	$ 4,601	1%
4	41%	$ 339,338	$ 16,967	$ 54,834	57%
1	15%	$ 90,344	$ 3,011	$ 90,344	no rev
2	4%	$ 153,878	$ 9,617	$ 76,989	154%
0	7%	$ 17,003	no qual. leads	no wins	no rev
0	0%	$ 10,266	no qual. leads	no wins	no rev
0	0%	$ 407,941	no qual. leads	no wins	no rev
0	0%	$ 22,000	no qual. leads	no wins	no rev
0	0%	$ —	no qual. leads	no wins	no rev
0	0%	$ —	no qual. leads	no wins	no rev
0	0%	$ —	no qual. leads	no wins	no rev
27	100%	$ 1,139,861	$ 9,499	$ 42,218	19%

mize your activities to hit a specific revenue target. The revenue target is fixed and the analysis focuses on optimizing the levers that drive total revenue and provides insight into marketing investment and hiring requirements. *Bottom-up analysis* is performed to determine the maximum revenue that can be attained by optimizing revenue drivers. Revenue is the dependent variable. This form of what-if analysis provides insight into the following:

~ How total revenue will be affected if we increase the probability of closing (e.g., enhance training or resource investment)
~ What type of return we will get if we invest more in this marketing activity (e.g., invest in labor or promotions to increase the number of leads)
~ What type of return we get if we increase the average deal size

Step 3: Forecast Monthly Lead Requirements

The final step of the ABM analysis is to forecast the number of new customer leads that are required per month, per sales process stage, to hit revenue targets. Modeling revenue distribution by quarter, average deal size, probability of conversion, cycle time, and cash flow recognition, the enterprise begins to get a clear picture of current performance and progress against business objectives. Using this lead forecasting approach, an enterprise will know well in advance whether marketing has insufficient leads in the pipeline to meet revenue targets. The obvious benefit is that with increased visibility, the management team will have additional time to course correct marketing initiatives, realign marketing investments, and get back on track to meeting targets.

10

OPTIMIZE MARKETING INVESTMENTS TO DRIVE PROFITABLE SALES

Every day, every marketer faces the critical decision of determining where to make marketing investments or—thinking more broadly—where to position marketing assets in order to drive profitable sales. Even if you've successfully developed a brand architecture that describes that combination of emotional and functional benefits that drive purchase intent for your brand, translated these benefits across the entire brand experience, and thus developed a brand experience blueprint, you're still not done. You still have to think about where to invest your marketing funds to drive sales.

The brand experience blueprint is just that—a blueprint of all of the potential customer interactions, ideally across both the current elements of the marketing mix, and all of the customer touch points. However, it doesn't tell you where you need to be investing your marketing dollars. It doesn't provide you with the creative spark that might be the basis of a market-based experiment. So even after applying a significant measure of science to your marketing efforts, there's still plenty of room to let your hair down and get creative.

The brand experience blueprint represents the marketer's laboratory and stands as the compendium of all your opportunities to communicate and engage your customers. This is where the experimentation can really begin, at least as it relates to identifying those tactics that might drive sales. By thinking horizontally, or even holistically, across the entire brand experience, the scientific marketer can identify those areas where marketing investment and experimentation make sense. The bottom line is that marketing has to invest in those campaigns and initiatives that drive sales. If an idea doesn't, then it's not worth your money.

This theory goes back to the premise of EMM. Part of bringing a scientific approach to how you invest in marketing is realizing that you will make mistakes. Too many marketers try to avoid even the possibility of making a mistake, tending to their sacred cows and staying on the safe, predictable path.

This isn't to say that safe and predictable decisions are necessarily good ones. On the contrary, these terrible decisions are all too acceptable. Outsourcing strategy to an advertising agency, continuing to support investment in marketing events, or paying for sponsorships that have no relationship to sales whatsoever are three examples of investments that conventional wisdom believes are safe—and real marketers believe are often heedlessly wasteful.

Marketers must bring an analytical approach, yes, but also a desire to apply the scientific method to what marketing does in an effort to continually increase knowledge of what drives sales and what doesn't. Unlike the traditional sciences, marketing is intimately connected to the enormously dynamic business marketplace. This means that what you learned last year might not be true next year. And this constant change makes the science of marketing terrifically exciting—as long as you're willing to adhere to the rigorous discipline required to learn what actually works and what doesn't.

For example, can the marketers in your company detail which investments pay out and which ones don't? Or, if that's not yet feasible, can they rank-order marketing mix investments to indicate which ones seem to perform better than others? At an even more elementary level, is there a simple record of investments and sales results?

Part of bringing a scientific discipline to marketing investing means applying the discipline from start to finish, not just waking up one day and deciding to apply ROI metrics to what's already been done. When you make a marketing investment, do you ask your marketing managers to create a financial profile of their proposed investment, indicating specifically where they expect to make cash outflows and also expect to see sales inflows? Think of it this way: This is exactly the sort of information you would demand if you were talking to your broker about where to invest your hard-earned money, regardless of risk. Why does your company deserve any less?

In making the decisions about where to invest marketing dollars, the marketer can use the brand experience blueprint as his or her portfolio, because it adequately lays out all of the current customer interactions in such a way as to communicate the brand's benefits. What levers should we pull for activating the brand? Where should we invest marketing dollars, either in marketing mix elements or in altering some current aspect of interaction across a customer touch point? Should we allow differentiation of offerings based on geography or targeted segment? All of these questions form part of the research and investigation that makes up the marketer's job. Granted, it's impossible for you to simply read a book and learn exactly where to make your marketing investments to drive the sales of your company. But you can learn the proper steps to follow and how to think through your approach to make the most of your marketing investments.

Generally speaking, every marketer should follow the same approach to making marketing investments, regardless of whether the investment is for launching a new product or for continuing to push your current offerings. This approach is relevant for every potential change or investment in the brand experience blueprint. Whether you're spending money to purchase advertising production and media, to create a more compelling customer extranet, or to ensure that your sales force communicates brand benefits, this approach works.

To drive profitable sales using EMM, marketers must take certain steps before even thinking of spending that first dollar:

1. Ensure *alignment* with the strategy that the marketing investment supports.
2. Identify where in the brand experience blueprint to make your marketing investment(s):

    a. Create the *marketing investment program*—marketing mix element or customer touch point.

    b. Develop a *profile of the investment and the return* on the marketing investment.

    c. Develop the nonfinancial metrics that are *likely leading indicators* of marketing return.

3. Implement the process or system that will let you *evaluate the progress* of your many investments, even before they're complete (prepare yourself to answer the question "Are we selling more?").

While it may be tempting to jump right in and make investment after marketing investment, that approach would abandon the heart of EMM's principles. A critical part of any investment is planning for what will happen, but equally as important is the necessity to measure what's happening and learn from it. What good is a winning marketing initiative that you're not able to repeat?

The appeal of this approach is that with every investment, you have the opportunity to get smarter, on individual, brand, and corporate levels. If the business model isn't in place to make this possible, then your marketing investment in learning is going to waste. You might hit a few home runs, but the loss of one key player will land you back in the cellar. Keep this in mind—learn from everything you do as a marketer. *Everything.*

ENSURE ALIGNMENT WITH THE BRAND ARCHITECTURE

Before even thinking about where to put your marketing investments, it's critical that you align potential marketing efforts with your brand architecture. While the emotional and functional benefits of your brand have presumably been incorporated into your brand experience blueprint, it's critical to make sure that every potential marketing program is synchronized and aligned with that same brand architecture.

While this may be as simple as reviewing your brand architecture before moving to the next step, many brands have to struggle with far more complex questions, like, say, How much does my brand vary from France to Japan? Which of my brand benefits are inviolable, and which ones are subject to interpretation?

The question that many marketers struggle with is how to make a particular brand architecture work in a local market. For example, given Pepto-Bismol's popularity in the Hispanic community, how should the brand architecture be applied differently in Latino markets as opposed to the broader U.S. market? Or if you're grappling with the age-old global versus local conundrum, how can the global brand manager ensure that a brand's positioning is applied consistently around the world, while giving the local marketers the leeway to make the brand's benefits relevant?

Figure 10.1 highlights the process trade-offs that any marketer must make when addressing such a challenge. The bottom line is that there are inevitably core elements of the brand architecture or core marketing processes as well as potentially regional/shared and localized elements. The placement of the dividing line must be driven by the inevitable investment trade-offs as determined by their ability to drive incremental sales. To answer our own question, the Pepto-Bismol brand architecture *is* the brand architecture. The leeway in interpretation will be driven by the specific return from investing in Latino-specific marketing.

Highly De-centralized	JAPAN	CANADA	U.S.A	FRANCE	GERMANY
Geographic Unit or Local Processes	Sales	Sales	Sales	Sales	Sales
	Research	Research	Research	Research	Research
	Pricing	Pricing	Pricing	Pricing	Pricing
Shared Processes	Promotions	Promotions		Promotions	Promotions
	Advertising	Advertising		Advertising	Advertising
Corporate or Global Processes	Marketing Recruiting & Training				
	Customer Service				
	Global Brand Strategy & Positioning & Trademark Compliance				
	Corporate Sponsorships & Marketing Alliances				
Highly Centralized	Product Development				

FIGURE 10.1   Positioning Brand Assets to Drive Profitable Sales

USE THE BRAND EXPERIENCE BLUEPRINT TO GUIDE YOUR MARKETING INVESTMENTS

Given all of the requirements of building a brand experience, it can seem daunting to determine how to best use marketing assets. In this instance, assets could include your time, your dollars, your brands, your sales force, your customer service reps—just about anything that you can leverage to improve your marketing position.

Marketers have a difficult time determining *where* across the brand experience to make investments and which element of the marketing mix or customer touch point should be included. How much do you spend on promotions, and how much on advertising? Should the available funds go toward developing new products or to support an improvement in customer service? There are so many competing priorities, and the addition of the customer touch points on top of the traditional elements of the marketing mix may at first overwhelm marketers. Don't worry—with EMM to help, you're not going to drown in options.

THE KEY TO SUCCESS: THINK HORIZONTALLY

Traditional marketers tend to spend an inordinate amount of money on projects such as advertising, promotions, and direct mail. It's time to reconsider spending for the sake of spending.

When you need to put your brand experience blueprint to work and choose your priorities, thinking horizontally means thinking across the entire brand experience, the way you would think about any networked decision. In other words, the fact that any relationship has numerous inflection points and opportunities for influence requires a marketer to think beyond the traditional domain of generating demand.

Many industrial companies have no real marketing capability and tend to think of marketing as little more than a production warehouse for annual reports or "brochure-ware" web sites. These companies also tend to combine marketing and sales under one roof, staffed by salespeople with less expertise in marketing.

Companies that have developed relatively sophisticated selling processes, usually supported by the CRM investments detailed in Chapter 5, look to marketing to fill the pipeline with leads or opportunities. In this instance, marketing makes investments that generate opportunities on which the sales force can then capitalize. The sales pipeline diagram shown in Figure 10.2 highlights how this approach generates rich opportunities to evaluate marketing investments. Marketers can track investments not only on their ability to generate opportunities, but also on the net output from the investment effort, meaning that all marketing investments can be tied downstream to specific sales generated by the lead.

Sales processes of this type are generally only useful for companies that fulfill products and services directly (e.g., financial services) as opposed to companies that sell through third parties or mass marketers (e.g., Kraft Foods).

This approach, which is already in place in many companies today, is certainly much better than leaving marketing unconnected to sales. But it still isn't optimal. While using the sales pipeline is an excellent way to evaluate the impact that marketing is having on sales, it has limited predictive value and looks at the enterprise very narrowly, giving marketing very little insight into the actual drivers of opportunities. It's a fine measurement system but a poor tool for deciding where to place investments.

What is important is that the data that make up the pipeline results help form your company's profile for specific marketing investments. In other words, the pipeline results help you understand the ability of certain marketing mix elements and certain marketing programs to drive profitable sales. It's a critical piece of your ongoing marketing learning and represents a primary method for gathering information about the effectiveness of your marketing.

While the pipeline is a great gauge of what works and what doesn't, it can't help you weigh all of your potential investment

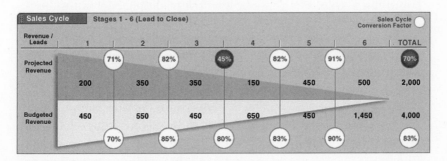

FIGURE 10.2   Sales Pipeline

options and opportunities. Its data will be factored into the decision, but you still need more.

The *more* in question requires evaluating all of the potential marketing investments across the brand experience blueprint. For every key customer, for every interaction, what are the potential marketing investments, and what is the profile of these potential investments?

The most sophisticated marketing organizations look across all customer interactions and then evaluate all of the potential marketing investments as part of a dynamic network. Highly sophisticated marketing organizations recognize the interdependence of every marketing investment and evaluate all investments together to determine how to optimize spending. Which marketing mix element works the best? Which element of the brand experience needs focus? Should you spend more money on promotions or invest in more call center capabilities? These trade-offs, for the most part, don't currently exist, since the predominant method of traditional marketing investment sits within the domain of traditional marketing departments.

Some marketers are weighing the trade-offs of investments in, say, advertising versus promotion versus packaging, but even then, it's rare that they evaluate these investments together in such a way as to estimate their combined effect. And in most cases, marketing doesn't play a role in many company decisions that affect customer touch points, so it's virtually impossible to bring the entire investment picture together.

In those rare companies where marketers bring a holistic view to investments in the marketing mix and investments in customer touch points, you can put numerous methods to work to *optimize* your marketing investments. This is the key to bringing the most scientific methods to bear on your total brand experience.

In the scientific community, optimization is defined as a mathematical methodology that allocates finite resources across multiple competitive, conflicting, and overlapping initiatives, each with unique constraints, to achieve an overall objective. Applied to the demand chain, optimization is a mathematical decision-making process that allocates finite resources across multiple channels, business constraints, and scenarios in order to determine the optimal mix of marketing investments to maximize return on marketing investment.

While this method of tracking investments may sound like

some kind of fantasy, chances are that your company is probably already using this sort of approach—just not anywhere near the marketing department. Your operations or logistics department might be using this method to determine the routing of your delivery trucks. Or your CFO or investment bank might be using it to model the ideal investment fund portfolio.

The concept of optimization is increasingly being applied to pricing, across all industries, but most recently migrating from strongholds such as airline tickets and hotel rooms to more traditional retail. The idea behind pricing optimization is quite simple: Different customers get different prices for the same product or service. Extrinsic drivers of pricing are taken into account (for airline tickets, channel used, advance purchase timing, Saturday night stay, etc.) and help the brand discriminate and improve overall revenue and profitability. See the Longs Drug Store case study later in this chapter to learn how pricing optimization could be happening at a drugstore near you.

CREATING A MARKETING INVESTMENT PROGRAM

The challenge of applying an optimization approach to marketing investments is that you have to get your hands on good input if you hope to make any use of the output. In order to create your marketing investment program, you need to first consider where you're headed.

> *Create the marketing investment program*
> *(your experiment), based on marketing mix element*
> *or customer touch point.*

The first step toward determining *where* to place your marketing assets is to develop a broad variety of potential marketing investments, looking at ways to activate your brand using both elements of the marketing mix and every customer touch point around the actual sale.

One of the drivers of the choices of investment should be the information that you might have gathered from previous investments. This profile should include not only descriptions, cash outflows, and cash inflows, but should also include components such as specific profiles of leads at each step in the sales process.

In other words, determine not just how many leads were created from a particular marketing investment, but also how many were converted at each stage of the sales process. Measuring quantity of opportunities generated by marketing is simply not sufficient. It's impossible to evaluate one marketing program against another unless there's a sense of potential return.

> **Develop a profile of the investment and the return on the Marketing investment.**

The need for potential return leads to the next required step: developing a detailed profile of the investment and, at the very least, an estimate of its possible return (see Figure 10.3). This is where the

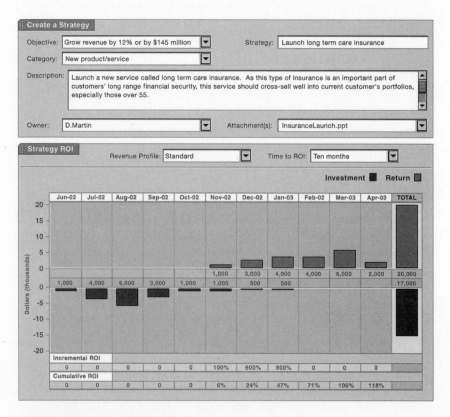

FIGURE 10.3   Marketing Investment Profile

rubber meets the road. Whether you're spending on billboards or on developing better scripts to drive the outbound teleselling, the only way to evaluate *where* in the brand experience to make investments is to put all of the investments on equal footing. Much as an investor might look at several potential investments and need to evaluate historical performance, volatility (beta), and numerous financial ratios (price/earnings, cash/share, return on equity, and so forth), so must a marketer put all marketing investments on equal footing.

The mere exercise of requiring marketing managers to treat all marketing spending as investments will pay almost immediate dividends in the caliber of the thought and approach applied to selling more stuff. You'll stop hearing rationalizations such as "Our awareness is way up, but our sales are still in the tank."

The idea here is not to require impossible accuracy, but to evaluate marketing investments against each other, so that you have all the cards in front of you. Part of having all the cards in front of you for decision making means having an ROI profile for each marketing investment. But even that's not enough. You'll need to dig deeper . . .

> **Develop the nonfinancial metrics that are likely leading indicators of marketing return.**

In addition to developing a financial profile for each potential marketing investment, marketers should identify those nonfinancial metrics that give a more complete picture of the potential investment and might also serve as leading indicators of the performance of the investment (see Figure 10.4).

These additional metrics can mean the difference between seizing a great opportunity and wasting a ton of money. Many marketers look at their marketing as if they were at the tables in Vegas. Once the money is spent, even if it's on media, they act as if the die is cast, nothing can be changed, and nothing is known until the money, leads, or opportunities roll in—or don't.

Inherent in every marketing investment is a set of assumptions. Just like any investment, there are numerous assumptions that drive the initial decision—and they can in turn drive the decision to up your bet if you're on a winning streak or fold and walk away from the table if the cards aren't going your way.

Direct Mail Joint Promo with AARP	Composite Market Score - 3, Revenue GAP - $2 Million		
Objective: Grow revenue by 12% or by $145 million	Tactic:		
Strategy: Launch Long Term Care Insurance	Direct Mail Joint Promo with AARP ▼		

Explanation of Gap	Sales Drivers (Components of Market Score)		
Driver Market Score ▲	Description ▲	Projected Actual ▲	Budgeted ▲
2	▶ Overall Sales Cycle Conversion Factor	70%	83%
3	▶ Actual Revenue to Date (000)	$500	$1,450
6	▶ Historical Tactic Performance	60-30-10	70-20-10
6	▶ Sales Force Perspective (4 point scale)	3.1	3.6
	1 - No Engagement		
	2 - Basic Awareness		
	3 - Thorough Understanding		
	4 - Complete Commitment		
7	▶ Total Distribution	$45,000	$525,000

FIGURE 10.4   Leading Indicators of Performance

For marketing investments, those assumptions might be as follows:

Sales cycle conversion factors

~ Any marketing investment that's tracked across the sales pipeline generates conversion factors at each step along the way (for instance, "The coupon generated 150 contacts; out of those, 65 percent visited the retail store; of those, 35 percent redeemed the coupon; and of those, 10 percent purchased an additional item").

~ These conversion factors form the heart of your company's CRM system and are an excellent leading indicator to determine whether your marketing investment is going to behave like similar investments that have preceded it.

Channel perspective

~ Despite what many marketers may think, your sales force is often your best proxy for determining how your customer might respond to your marketing investments. Your sales force or your distributors might be able to vote on the effectiveness of your marketing investment even before you've put it in the field. The key here is to tie such input to historical results, just to make sure that your channel is aligned with the way your customer thinks.

Investment risk (beta)

~ It's important to capture some of the intangible qualities of those marketing investments that are difficult to measure. In this instance, investigate opportunities for creating your own evaluation system that would introduce a risk measurement, thereby capturing a number of the unstated elements of the marketing investment. Ask marketers if one investment is riskier than another, and they will most likely give you their gut reaction. The problem is that very little of this intuition is captured anywhere or incorporated into broader investment decisions. This evaluation of up-front risk can play a critical part in determining where to place investments.

Historical performance

~ While you might be making a particular marketing investment for the first time in a market or behind a particular brand, the company's experience with the investment vehicle should be taken into account. If the company gets a good response from print ads or is able to drive retail traffic from Web-based coupons, then this historical ability should weigh on the decision making. Access to this historical perspective should also help generate *real* risk measures based on actual performance instead of just gut measurement.

> *Implement the process/system that will let you evaluate the progress of your many experiments even before they're complete (and answer the question "Are we selling more?").*

A key element of positioning your marketing assets to drive profitable sales is having the right systems in place to know when you're actually being successful. Most marketers follow several or even all of these steps, but are at a loss when it comes to actually knowing what's working and what's not. As discussed in Chapter 3, this is why it's critical to plug marketing into finance and into the enterprise systems that most companies have purchased and implemented over the past decade.

Even if you don't have fancy systems or a big IT department, you can cobble together this information on a regular basis to determine the state of your marketing investments: How's your portfolio doing? Are you making money?

Marketers can't just sit around and complain that there's no way to track this or track that and throw up their hands. Part of practicing EMM means creating the measures and information-gathering capabilities that will let you know the results of your investments. Staying on top of their progress can mean the difference between making your numbers and missing them by a mile.

Why is this? Because when you invest in marketing, you often have the opportunity to reevaluate in midstream. As Figure 10.5 illustrates, you can evaluate how your investment is faring against your original budget and, in essence, rethink whether it's the best allocation of money at any particular point in time. Much as investors rethink their portfolio positions on a regular basis, so too should you bring the same rigor to your company's investments.

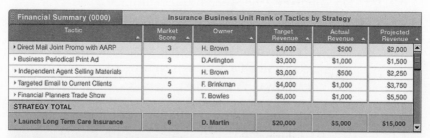

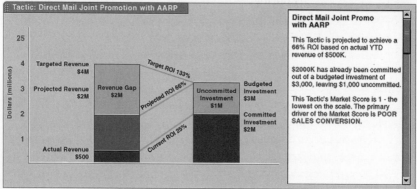

FIGURE 10.5   Evaluate Investment Return Continuously

Armed with a process to measure the impact of your marketing investments, you'll have everything you need to practice EMM when positioning your marketing assets to drive profitable sales.

At the end of the day, you have to be prepared to answer the simple question, "Am I selling more stuff?," as it relates to any of your marketing investments, and then make necessary changes accordingly. The decision of where to place your marketing assets is driven largely by the quality of the information that you have, the rigor that you bring to the decision, and the processes that you've built over time to learn from all of the decisions that have gone before. And the past is prologue—what you learned yesterday will help you today, and what you learn today will drive your revenues higher tomorrow.

CASE STUDY: Longs Drug Store

USING PRICING OPTIMIZATION TO DRIVE IMMEDIATE SALES RESULTS

Longs Drug Stores Corporation (NYSE:LDG) is the nation's sixth-largest drugstore chain. Founded in 1938 by brothers Joe and Tom Long as Longs Self-Service Drugs, the company currently operates stores in California, Hawaii, Washington, Nevada, Colorado, and Oregon. Each store averages annual sales in excess of $9.5 million.

Longs has more than 440 stores and recorded approximately $4.3 billion in sales during 2002. This represented a modest 4 percent increase over 2001, but was dwarfed by sales of the drugstore industry leader Walgreen Co., which reported $24.8 billion in sales during 2001 at its 3,706 stores nationwide. Overall pharmacy sales in the United States were $165.2 billion last year. Longs' performance for fiscal 2002, which ended January 31, was generally disappointing. The true barometer of growth, same-store sales, lagged behind the best performers, and margins were low.

How is Longs different from Walgreens? Longs stores tend to be much larger, upward of 10,000 square feet compared to the smaller, 5,000-square-foot Walgreens stores. While Longs stores tend to be in suburban strip malls, Walgreens has focused on placing its stores on busy streets.

More important, Walgreens has traditionally been a leader in implementation of new technologies to drive retail operations. It was the first drugstore chain to equip stores with VSAT satellite communication and install point-of-sale scanning chainwide. These investments have paid dividends over the years and have helped Walgreens thrive amid ferocious competition. Longs has been relatively late in making such technology investments and is now in the unfortunate role of playing catch-up.

In the past few years, observers say, Longs has struggled to deal with outdated technology that contributed to inventory control problems at its warehouses and resultant difficulties in fulfilling individual store orders. When you're playing the game against industry giants, including some best-in-class players (Wal-Mart, Walgreens), then you can't afford to be playing with old equipment.

Because Longs is grappling with how to compete with much larger chains of stores, such as Walgreens and CVS, in addition to the category competition from large grocery stores and mass merchandisers (Wal-Mart, Target), it has to identify those investments that drive immediate results. It's not likely to stay out of the consolidation game, unless it's able to grow more quickly. One area in which Longs has seen and acted on an opportunity is pricing.

Most retailers price their items and determine markdowns based on gut feelings, with some thought given to individual store perspectives or the experience of their merchandisers or store managers. They generally set their prices one of three ways: marking up from cost, benchmarking against the competition's prices, or simply playing a hunch. This lack of a scientific approach is remarkable, given the precise data available and the ease of making a connection between what marketers and merchandisers do and what the end results are.

The cost and complexity of crunching all pricing data to determine the *optimal* price for every stockkeeping unit (SKU) based on the critical variables chosen—location, inventory level, weather—have historically prevented retailers from taking such hands-on analytical action. But thanks to the development of specific software that builds on the learning reservoirs of yield management programs pioneered by the airline industry, price optimization programs are now available to retailers.

These software programs, which gather and analyze the enormous quantities of data that now sit in point-of-sale and ERP systems, leverage probability algorithms to come up with an individual demand curve for each product in each retail store. With this information in hand, retailers can identify which products are most price sensitive. Then they can adjust prices up or down according to each store's priorities—profit, revenue, or market share—to achieve, in theory, a maximum profit margin.

Longs Drug Stores Corporation has embarked on just such an effort, putting pricing optimization to work in its retail locations in an effort to drive overall profitability. From a consumer perspective, one interesting outcome of implementing price optimization at the retail level is that prices at the shelf could be different in different retail locations, as is the case with airline tickets. Also, prices that normally ended in familiar digits—.99 or .95—are replaced with odd amounts like $3.21 and $6.36.

In addition to developing a demand curve for every item in every store, these software programs can also forecast price and promotion sensitivities for every item in every store, thereby helping to determine how to best execute strategies to drive profitable sales. DemandTec developed Longs' price optimization software; other competitors in this space include KhiMetrics, KSS, Spotlight Solutions, and ProfitLogix.

Longs is delighted with its results and has expanded its initial test of the pricing optimization software to the majority of its retail locations. Terry Burnside, chief operating officer of Longs Drug Stores, notes that the technology has brought about a "category-by-category increase in sales and margins," particularly in nonpharmacy sales, which generate most of Longs' profits.

However, just implementing the software is only part of the necessary investment. Retailers have to ensure that their business models are adjusted accordingly—that is, integrating the pricing software with shelf pricing mechanisms and each store's point-of-sale system to ensure that scanners record accurate prices. Further down the value chain, retailers can compile knowledge gained from pricing optimization software to inform decisions and communications about additional orders. There are, of course, cultural changes as well—the most significant of which is the requirement that existing employees have faith that the system will deliver the profits, despite the quirky prices.

"Optimizing OTC [over-the-counter] pricing strategies is an important part of the company's growth and overall business performance," said the CEO of Longs. "We anticipate this [pricing optimization] implementation will help us improve our profitability, yet allow us to maintain or improve our competitive price image with our customers." If Longs isn't able to grow, it's likely to become an acquisition candidate for some of the larger players. Unfortunately, standing still and not generating ever higher sales and profits is not the way to survive in the competitive drugstore business.

Even the acquisition prospects for the company are dubious. Walgreens has a proud tradition of not growing by acquisition, so they're unlikely to purchase a company like Longs. Other players, such as Rite Aid, are still digesting many previous acquisitions and working through issues such as regulatory scandals. The slow demise of Kmart, another company that has a long history of being outspent on technology, comes to mind for Longs shareholders. Is this going to be a similar ride?

Longs' approach of leveraging optimization is at least giving its sales a shot in the arm. Ironically, retailers have spent comparative fortunes in making sure that their inventories are managed flawlessly, their logistics efforts are as efficient as possible, and their employees are managed closely. What they've not put nearly enough effort into is how to leverage marketing to drive profitable sales higher. You're not winning the game unless you can continue to grow sales in your existing stores. Pricing optimization offers a window into how the power of optimization can be applied to businesses and make an impact almost immediately.

MARKETER'S SCIENTIFIC METHOD: OPTIMIZING MARKETING INVESTMENTS

Following are the steps to take in order to optimize your marketing investments.

Step 1. Ensure Alignment with the Strategy That the Marketing Investment Supports

While the strategy might be clear in the CMO's head, it's often not clear throughout the marketing organization or even in the minds of the marketing staff responsible for the details of a particular marketing investment. Making this alignment happen can go a long way to avoiding off-strategy investments, also known as wasted money.

Step 2. Identify Where in the Brand Experience Blueprint to Make Your Marketing Investment(s)

~ Create the *marketing investment program* (your experiment)—the marketing mix element or customer touch point. Language can have a powerful impact on the way marketing happens and how it's perceived in your company. The more you talk about marketing investments and actually follow up on them with financial rigor, the more likely EMM will gain followers outside of marketing.

~ Develop a *profile of the investment and the return* on the marketing investment. Remember that you get what you measure, so if you're not even making an educated guess at the investment profile for where you put marketing dollars, you'll never get any smarter.

~ Develop the nonfinancial metrics that are *likely leading indicators* of marketing return. Because your marketing investment may require a significant investment before and during the actual return, the smarter you are at identifying other potential indicators of results, the better your decisions will be. Just as with stock market investments, what are those leading indicators for your marketing investments?

Step 3. Implement the Process/System to Evaluate the Progress of Your Experiments before They're Complete

In other words, be able to answer the question "Are we selling more?" You're condemned to staying in the dark until you put the right systems in place to manage your marketing investments. Systems don't have to be backed by million-dollar investments in information technology. The right process could consist of spreadsheets and meetings.

CONCLUSION: A NEW DAY
FOR MARKETING

Now that you've reached the end, don't forget how you got here. Marketing's bad habits are deeply ingrained; take the time to drag them out into the light. It's a new day for marketing, and it begins with clearing out the dead wood and taking full advantage of what you already have.

WHY IS NOW THE TIME TO BEGIN PRACTICING ENTERPRISE MARKETING MANAGEMENT?

Simply put, the market forces of competition and innovation are fueling the evolution and adoption of scientific marketing practices, including the following key drivers:

~ **Increasing market complexity.** Market fragmentation, channel and customer touch point proliferation, and globalization have combined to create a substantially more complex marketing environment. By helping to develop and implement standard, repeatable processes, marketing business applications help manage the planning, execution, and measurement of marketing activities.

211

~ **Accelerating demand for speed to market.**   As competitive pressures increase, the window of opportunity for new products and services is narrowing. As a result, marketers face increasing pressure to reduce product and market development cycles. Scientific marketing business applications support and foster collaboration, making marketing best practices and project management processes readily available to marketers and their internal and external service providers.

~ **Growing need to capture marketing knowledge.** Increasing dispersion and turnover of marketing personnel put pressure on the ability of enterprises to actually use the intellectual capital they've built up over years. Customer relationship management (CRM) and enterprise resource planning (ERP) applications aid in the execution and measurement of marketing efforts, but ongoing improvement requires an institutional memory to leverage successes and avoid programs with lackluster performance. In general, marketing remains an island in most enterprises today, disconnected from many of the core business processes and corresponding information flows—such as sales, service, manufacturing, and finance—limiting accessibility and collaboration, both within the enterprise and beyond the enterprise to critical service providers.

~ **Increasing availability of innovative marketing technologies.**   Early adopters and developers of scientific marketing applications and technologies are mostly using these capabilities to help manage the development of marketing-related content, automate work flow, and offer some integration with front- and back-office applications. But these early-stage applications are just the tip of the iceberg. The coming years will see the large-scale adoption and implementation of scientific marketing applications, which will give an enterprise the functionality necessary to plan, coordinate, and measure the business impact of their branding and marketing efforts. Enterprise marketing management (EMM) and the new science of marketing, as a set of business applications and disciplines, will evolve to a holistic approach that addresses a broad array of marketer pain points, including:

- ○ Understanding customers, channel partners, and end consumers
- ○ Understanding markets
- ○ Brand management
- ○ Project/campaign management
- ○ Integrated support for selling channels, direct sales, and service operations
- ○ Evaluation, measurement, and knowledge capture from marketing programs

~ **Escalating demand for marketing efficiency and effectiveness.**   Enterprises are under increasing pressure to deliver short-term profits while fostering enduring growth. With marketing expenditures reaching 15 to 35 percent of overall revenue, marketers face increasing scrutiny to be more accountable and to optimize return on marketing investment (ROMI) and return on marketing assets (ROMA).

WHAT WILL IT TAKE FOR ENTERPRISES TO SUCCEED WITH THEIR MARKETING EFFORTS?

The only way for marketers to succeed in the current environment is to embrace the scientific methods in this book and get their hands dirty with the business of selling more, more, more. To help guide you along the way, keep in mind the key principles listed in the summary table that follows:

Summary Table Guiding Principles of Enterprise Marketing Management

Part	Guiding Principles	From	To
I	1. Marketing is a science, not an art.	• Marketing as an art	• Marketing as science
	2. Architect your brand.	• Brands as identity campaigns	• Brands as business
	3. Plug marketing into enterprise.	• Disconnected and event driven	• Connected and outcome driven
II	4. Take ownership of the brand experience	• Interactions and transactions	• Sustain brand preference
	5. Plug marketing into CRM.	• Customer relationships	• Brand experiences
	6. Cross-market to cross-sell.	• Customer acquisition focus	• Customer penetration focus
	7. Use new media for new action.	• Pulling awareness levers	• Pulling activation levers
III	8. Restructure based on brand experience.	• "Make-centered" operations	• "Sell-centered" operations
	9. Measure investment performance.	• Expense and earn	• Investment and annuity
	10. Optimize marketing investments.	• Static investment decisions	• Dynamic, optimized decisions

You've got a lot to tackle if you're going to put enterprise marketing management into place in your business. You have to develop a deep understanding—a scientific understanding—of your market and your customers. Only then can you adequately develop your brand's architecture and find the best way to communicate it to your customers to make them buy your product rather than just "feel good" about it.

Every asset must be considered a marketing asset. Charlemagne, ruler of France, when conjuring up how he thought he would combat his enemies with limited resources, once uttered, "Let my armies be the rocks and trees and the birds in the sky."

So must you look beyond the traditional elements of the marketing mix to win in your markets. Let your marketers be every member of your sales force, every customer service rep, every e-mail, every invoice, every voice mail, every interaction with every customer at any time. Driving sales higher and outsmarting your competitors means that your brand can't just live in traditional communication vehicles.

Your brand must come alive as an *experience* for every customer. The longer you delay in understanding what that experience is today and how you should optimize it, the longer you delay moving to the next level of sales and profits.

But, once you've developed that brand experience, you've simply created the plan that needs to be executed. The market battle can't be won with just a great strategy. You have to build the infrastructure to make it possible and you have to execute in the field to deliver real brand benefits, real value to your customers. Part of today's challenge is that this brand experience happens largely by chance.

Companies spend fortunes on developing new products, making sure that there are enough salespeople to service customers, investing in production capacity, and managing cash flow closely. No marketing mix detail is too picayune for marketing's attention—whether it's the process color of the sales brochures or the placement of the tag line on the package.

Meanwhile, the total brand experience is not being actively managed by anyone. The bottom line: Marketing must do more and take complete ownership of the brand experience. Quite simply, no one else will.

That's to say nothing of the need to mobilize the rest of the company to evangelize the benefits that drive sales. Today, marketing seems to have a hard time just getting its own story straight. Without investments in infrastructure, such as CRM systems that help marketing drive how customer service reps respond to specific customer interactions, the rest of the company doesn't have a prayer of keeping to the message.

Keeping to the message is just the start. You have to crawl before you walk. It may be nice to just get everyone on the same message, but the more advanced companies out there have to think about how to sell a portfolio of products and services, not just sell the same thing over and over again. Figuring out how to get a customer to cross-buy is marketing's job, but it's actually up to the rest of the company to make it happen.

Unless you're working in a new media environment, where the brand experience and the sales transaction happen in the same place, marketing has to rely on sales or customer service in most instances to ensure that cross-buying actually occurs. Rote memorization of "would you like fries with that?" can only go so far, so marketing has to raise the capabilities of everyone who interacts with customers if it hopes to cross-sell against the status quo.

Once you've got your plans in place for taking ownership of the brand experience, you have to make sure that you've actually built the ability to manage it. Where are you going to place your investments? Which ones are working and which ones are not?

Surprisingly, things that we can all access for free about our own investment portfolios are nearly impossible to access for a company's marketing investments. What's the risk of this investment? What's the cash flow profile of this investment? How have we done in investments like this in the past?

Admit it. At some time in your career, you've sat around a table of decision makers and had to make a leap of faith on marketing investments because you didn't have the information infrastructure in place to treat marketing like an investment. You've essentially decided that you can live with such an enormous risk to your company's well-being.

We have to admit it. The EMM road is the more difficult road to take. It brings strict accountability, requires real work to make marketing a legitimate discipline, forces you to take responsibility for the success of the entire enterprise, and makes you get out of your comfort zone and harness the assets of the company, not just manage vendors who tend to laugh a bit too loudly at your jokes.

Now that you've gotten this far, it's plain to see that marketing is indeed not an art, it is a science. If you've been looking for a way to reinvent marketing at your company, now you know what to do. And if you're short on scientific marketing expertise and need some help putting enterprise marketing management to work for your company, help is just a click away at www.marketingscientists.com.

What are you waiting for?

INDEX

219